FORMULA 1.
CREATING THE SPECTACLE

FORMULA 1
CREATING THE SPECTACLE

ALAN HENRY

HAZLETON PUBLISHING

publisher
RICHARD POULTER

production manager
STEVEN PALMER

managing editor
PETER LOVERING

publishing development manager
SIMON MAURICE

business development manager
SIMON SANDERSON

sales promotion
CLARE KRISTENSEN

art editor
STEVE SMALL

photography by
BRYN WILLIAMS

First published in 1998

ISBN 1-874557-63-2

Printed in Hong Kong through World Print

ACKNOWLEDGEMENTS
Many people working on the inside of the Grand Prix business have assisted me in researching what I hope the reader will find an absorbing insight into this complex and highly demanding sport. In particular I would like to thank Trevor Foster and Ian Phillips of Jordan Grand Prix, Ron Dennis and Jo Ramirez of McLaren International, David Richards and the Benetton F1 team and Alistair Watkins of the FIA's media department.

My appreciation is also due to Bryn Williams for carrying out much of the photo research for this volume as well as actually supplying all the shots which appear between its covers.

A.H.

distributors

UNITED KINGDOM	NORTH AMERICA	AUSTRALIA	NEW ZEALAND	SOUTH AFRICA
Biblios Ltd	Motorbooks International	Technical Book and Magazine	David Bateman Ltd	Motorbooks
Star Road	PO Box 1, 729 Prospect Ave.	Co. Pty	PO Box 100-242	341 Jan Smuts Avenue
Partridge Green	Osceola	295 Swanston Street	North Shore Mail Centre	Craighall Park
West Sussex RH13 8LD	Wisconsin 54020, USA	Melbourne, Victoria 3000	Auckland 1330	Johannesburg
Tel: 01403 710971	Tel: (1) 715 294 3345	Tel: (03) 9663 3951	Tel: (9) 415 7664	Tel: (011) 325 4458/60
Fax: 01403 711143	Fax: (1) 715 294 4448	Fax: (03) 9663 2094	Fax: (9) 415 8892	Fax: (011) 325 4146

CONTENTS

INTRODUCTION

This volume is intended to take the reader on a trip behind the scenes of one of the most complex and intriguing professional sports in the world. Grand Prix motor racing exerts a compelling hold on armies of committed fans and casual viewers around the globe thanks to the all-seeing eye of the television cameras which have transformed the whole business over the past 25 years.

The FIA Formula 1 World Championship depends for its success on a large number of highly committed, single-minded individuals to whom perfection is only just about good enough. The fascination which comes with their involvement, and the diversity of the tasks involved in keeping the whole global show on the road, form the central themes of what is, in essence, an ever-changing story.

Within these pages you will read about how the cars are transported to the races, how they are scrutineered, how the timing system works, and the practice, qualifying and race procedures as well as how the individual competing teams organise themselves backstage. The drivers may be the glittering stars of the show, but they are supported by a cast of thousands. I hope this stands as a tribute to their unceasing efforts.

Alan Henry,
Tillingham, Essex,
July 1998

chapter 1

A GLOBAL CHALLENGE

Grand Prix motor racing has evolved over fifty years into possibly the biggest regularly staged global sport, now attracting television audiences which are exceeded only by those for the Olympic Games and football's World Cup.

Of course those two last-mentioned sporting epics are held only once every four years, yet the FIA Formula 1 World Championship takes place, pretty well at fortnightly intervals, across at least 16 races on an annual basis. The sport is governed by the Paris-based Fédération Internationale de l'Automobile, which owns the commercial rights to the contest, but the exploitation and management of those rights have been granted to a company called Formula One Administration run by a compact, dynamic businessman named Bernard Ecclestone.

A glance down any F1 pit lane across the world offers a testament to Ecclestone's far-sightedness. Thirty years ago Grand Prix racing was a slightly haphazard affair in which organisers never quite knew how many cars would appear for their particular events and mechanics worked in conditions of near-squalor, sometimes with scarcely any protection from the elements, in gravel-strewn paddock areas.

Contrast those distant memories with the well-drilled ranks of immaculate transporters drawn up behind the purpose-built pit lane garages of the 1990s and you can see just how dramatically the F1 business has been transformed. And the new wealth that has been injected into the sport as a direct result of this transformation is only a small part of the story.

Opposite: International flair. Australia joined the Grand Prix trail as recently as 1985, but its race is already regarded as one of the most prestigious on the calendar. This is the start/finish straight at Melbourne's Albert Park circuit, to which the race was switched from Adelaide in 1996.

Above: The impressive array of transporters lined up behind the pit garages.

Evolution of F1's Television Age

The reality is that the story of F1's global expansion is the story of Bernie Ecclestone's rise to multi-millionaire status. In 1998 the *Sunday Times* newspaper rated him the sixth-richest man in Britain with an accumulated wealth of around £1.5 billion. Any account of how Grand Prix racing has operated over the past three decades necessarily requires an explanation of how he came to fill this pivotal role.

In a nutshell, Ecclestone has scaled these spectacular heights of business success by having the foresight to exploit and understand the television coverage potential offered by Grand Prix motor racing. In his current position as Vice-President, Promotional Affairs of the FIA, he is the most powerful man in world motor racing. Some people would claim he is even the most powerful man in world sport. An energetic, trim 67-year-old, he knows everybody and everything that goes on within F1, operating his empire at the race tracks from a discreet silver-grey motorhome in the paddocks across Europe.

By any standards Ecclestone is a fascinating character. On the one hand he can be a ruthless negotiator, deploying a brain power and intellect which few can rival in any business sphere. On the other, he can be one of the boys when among those on the inside of motor racing whom he has known for a long time. He will get richer still if digital television coverage in Europe really takes off over the next few years, poised to reap the benefits of a £40 million investment in a 'portable' television studio which is transported round the world simply to handle the digital coverage. His F1 Administration organisation, together with FOCA Communications, now employs over 200 people and he has purchased a BAe 146 60-seater jet airliner to transport those required to the European races.

Opposite: The essence of Formula 1. Michael Schumacher's Ferrari F300 swings through the Massenet left-hander at Monaco during practice for the most glamorous race on the calendar.

Left: Bernie Ecclestone hears how it is from Michael Schumacher.

So where did all this start? Bernie was born in 1931, the son of a trawler captain from Suffolk. His interest in motor racing stretched back to the immediate post-war years when he raced a motor cycle on the grass track at Brands Hatch when he was only a teenager.

Later he would become an active and enthusiastic car racer, first at the wheel of a Formula 3 Cooper, later with a Cooper-Bristol single-seater and a Cooper-Jaguar sports car. In 1958 he made an unsuccessful attempt to qualify a Connaught for the Monaco Grand Prix, by which time he was managing the interests of the British driver Stuart Lewis-Evans, who was driving in the Vanwall team alongside Stirling Moss and Tony Brooks.

After Lewis-Evans sadly suffered what were to prove fatal burns when he crashed in the 1958 Moroccan Grand Prix, Bernie dropped out of racing to concentrate on his business interests. When he reappeared on the scene eight years later, he took up as business manager of the late Jochen Rindt, who was killed at Monza practising for the 1970 Italian Grand Prix at the wheel of a Lotus 72.

Bernie was a close friend of Jochen and the Austrian driver's death deeply affected him. It is therefore nice to record that the Rindt family's links with F1 continue to this day through Jochen's daughter Natascha, now 30, who works for FOCA TV at the races. Bernie had also been a partner with her father in Jochen Rindt Racing, the semi-works Lotus Formula 2 team, and continued running those cars briefly through the winter of 1970/71 in the immediate aftermath of Jochen's death.

However, Bernie, who had made a success of the motor cycle and car sales business as well as some shrewd and timely property dealings, by now harboured more lavish ambitions. He was to purchase the Brabham Formula 1 team from its co-founder Ron Tauranac and took control at the start of 1972, placing his foot firmly on the bottom step of a ladder which would eventually carry him to multi-millionaire status.

Distinguished motor cycle champion John Surtees recalls being taken by his father to buy motor cycle parts from Bernie's family home in the early post-war years, the future Brabham boss apparently operating out of his mother's kitchen at the time. Although Bernie actually trained as a chemist, his true talents proved to be as a dealer and the world of commerce was destined to take him a long way from his modest beginnings in life.

'Ron Tauranac had initially spoken to me as early as the 1971 Monaco Grand Prix about the prospect of getting involved with him in the Brabham team,' he recalled, 'but negotiations were not completed until later that year. Ron initially asked me if I could give him some help on the business side, but later he said, "I think I want to sell, do you want to buy half?"

'I told him that I didn't particularly want to buy half, but if he wanted to sell, then I would be prepared to buy the whole business.' Which is what he eventually did.

The original idea was that Tauranac should stay on in a consultancy role, but Bernie found that it just didn't work out. 'Ultimately, you couldn't really employ anybody who had once owned the company,' he reflected. 'It wasn't good for him and it wasn't good for me.'

In his new role as team owner, Ecclestone would soon emerge as a leading light in the F1 Constructors' Association. He had the time and mental agility necessary to do all the time-consuming negotiations with race organisers, so it was no surprise that the other team owners were happy to elect him President of FOCA.

Ecclestone also took the financial risk involved in staging some of the more commercially precarious races in the late 1970s. The other teams were not interested in taking those risks, so Bernie willingly gambled. And took any profit which was going.

Meanwhile, the Brabham team was thriving under Ecclestone's control. By 1973 the young South African designer Gordon Murray was in firm charge on the technical side and developed the BT44

International exposure. Sponsors such as Winfield pay a huge amount for their F1 involvement and maximise it in every way possible. The immaculate Williams transporters keep the message clear away from the circuits. Benson & Hedges is now closely identified with the Jordan team while FedEx and Mild Seven keep the Benettons fuelled with finance.

Ferrari, the most famous and prestigious name – and marketing brand – in the F1 business.

and BT44B generation of F1 challengers which would win races over two seasons in the hands of Carlos Reutemann and Carlos Pace.

No question about it, Bernie was an exacting employer, insisting that the race shop at the Brabham factory should be kept as tidy as possible. Sometimes he would pick up a broom and do a bit of sweeping himself, but more often somebody would be in deep trouble if they did not get the job done to his high standards.

On the other hand, he was shrewd enough to realise that Murray was an unusually talented designer and he was always prepared to spend money to make the Brabham cars go faster. In that respect, Bernie was extremely pragmatic: the better the cars went, the more success they would achieve and the richer he would become on the back of that success.

Today's F1 television coverage has achieved global levels of exposure which would have seemed remarkable – perhaps even unbelievable – two decades ago. Did he really anticipate the potential of this hidden F1 asset when he bought the Brabham team in 1971?

'No, definitely not,' he explained many years later, albeit with a modesty which was not totally convincing. 'I wasn't thinking in those terms at all when I bought Brabham. It was only when I began to get fully involved in the whole scene that I appreciated just how fragmented the television coverage had been.

'Some people covered a few races, some people none at all. My initial motivation was to get the whole business grouped together in an effort to get some decent overall coverage.'

By the start of 1976 the Brabham team had subtly changed its emphasis. No longer did Ecclestone pay to use customer Cosworth DFV engines, but instead forged a deal with Alfa Romeo for a supply of its powerful but heavy flat-12 engines. Alfa also paid handsomely for the privilege of equipping Brabham – and two years later Ecclestone replaced Martini as the team's title sponsor with the Italian dairy company Parmalat. They would remain on the flanks of the Brabhams for almost ten years.

By 1979 it was clear that Ecclestone and the FOCA-aligned teams were in a strong position to stake a claim to a larger share of the television income which, on the face of it, accrued to the sport's governing body, then known as FISA. Yet it was Bernie's tireless efforts which had generated all this income for the sport and, quite rightly, FOCA felt it was worth a larger slice of the cake.

For their part, the governing body did not like what they saw. Ecclestone and FOCA, they reasoned, were having too much commercial influence. The whole affair was aggravated in 1979 when the newly elected FISA President, Jean-Marie Balestre, decided to take on FOCA, determined to retrieve for FISA the notional concept of 'sporting power'.

Ecclestone now led his FOCA-aligned teams into a battle over the fundamental matter of who controlled motor racing. It was a turbulent period in the sport's history with races being boycotted, and others taking place outside the official World Championship.

Yet Bernie continued to remain the most influential man in the F1 pit lane. FOCA and FISA eventually reached an accommodation which was enshrined in the Concorde Agreement, a complex protocol of rules and regulations which was originally framed to control the way in which the sport was administered from a technical, financial and sporting viewpoint. Yet the most important single long-term result to stem from the FOCA/FISA wars, as they became known, was the emergence of Ecclestone's legal adviser Max Mosley as one of the behind-the-scenes power brokers.

As F1 became more popular throughout the 1980s, and Ecclestone became progressively richer, so Mosley laid the foundations of his own personal challenge for power on the international motor-sporting scene. In 1991, after a carefully judged campaign, Mosley defeated Balestre for the FIA

FIA President Max Mosley *(left)* and Ecclestone are the two most powerful individuals in this huge global sport.

Presidency. The governing body would eventually devolve the right to exploit the commercial aspects of the F1 World Championship to Ecclestone's companies, which would make him even richer in the longer term.

The Concorde Agreement was renewed several times, but by 1997 three teams – Williams, McLaren and Tyrrell – stood out against signing a new deal simply because they felt that Ecclestone's business organisation was taking too big a slice of the commercial cake. This provoked an impasse which was not resolved until the 1998 Monaco Grand Prix, by which time Ecclestone's business empire was under fire from the tenacious European Union Competition Commissioner, one Karel van Miert.

Van Miert's initial contention was that the television coverage contracts held by Ecclestone's companies are illegal under EU law because they were not awarded after a process of open-market tendering.

Prior to Monaco '98, those teams which had signed the 1997 version of the Concorde Agreement – Ferrari, Benetton, Jordan, Sauber, Minardi, Arrows and Prost – enjoyed a seven-way split of a fixed percentage of the gross television revenue. This money was payable whether or not the Commercial Rights Holder – in this case Bernie Ecclestone – made a profit on the overall operation of the various television coverage contracts through his FOCA TV organisation and associated subsidiaries.

In exchange, those teams would agree to enter the FIA Formula One World Championship for a period of ten years. Eventually McLaren, Williams and Tyrrell joined in and the 1998 Concorde Agreement was duly finalised – guaranteeing individual teams between $9.8 and $23 million (US) in annual television income. It was not exactly a licence to print money, but from the summer of 1998, buttressed by this income stream, you needed to be a pretty inept manager if your F1 team was to go bust.

For his part, Mosley never had any doubts that most F1 teams would be significantly better off under the terms of the proposed new Concorde Agreement.

'The changes to the division of the television money which have followed the revised Agreement have had a fundamental effect on the smaller signatory teams,' said Max, 'in that the amount of money they can expect to receive has been significantly increased.

'Under the previous Concorde Agreement, the FIA would make an agreement with the teams which, in turn, would reach an agreement with the Commercial Rights Holder [Ecclestone]. Now, instead of a straight line, what we have is effectively a triangle. The FIA has agreements with both Mr Ecclestone and the teams. Part of each of these two agreements provides that the Commercial Rights Holder will pay the teams the moneys as laid down in the Concorde Agreement.'

There are two key issues which the dissenting teams continue to be worried about. They do not believe they are receiving sufficient TV income and they are concerned about who will run the commercial side of F1 when the time comes for Bernie Ecclestone to retire. However, Mosley remains reluctant to reveal what proportion of the moneys are taken by Ecclestone in his role as Commercial Rights Holder.

'It is impossible to quote the precise sums,' he says, 'because so many of the deals are to do with television, an area which is going through significant expansion at the moment. This will be to the considerable benefit of the teams. In this area, the financial expenditure is enormous. I believe that Mr Ecclestone now has 140 people working on producing elements of the TV show, whereas in 1989 I believe there were only five.

'Notwithstanding that, the arrangement made by the teams is that they take a percentage of the gross. Two or three years ago, Mr Ecclestone made an enormous investment in digital television at a time when almost everyone was saying that he would lose every penny. It is now looking as though digital TV will be a great success. That's good for him, but it is even better for the teams because,

Opposite, top: Paddock gossip. Team owner Eddie Jordan shares a secret with his commercial director Ian Phillips.

Opposite, bottom: Power brokers. McLaren MD Ron Dennis *(left)* in company with his technical director Adrian Newey.

No eavesdropping! You can be sure that whatever Bernie Ecclestone *(right)* is saying to Eddie Jordan is private and confidential.

although they took no risk at all, they don't have to meet any of the costs involved.

'It is my view that the arrangements are more than fair to the teams. The best evidence that I can offer of this is that of the 11 teams, when they were all offered the opportunity to withdraw and re-negotiate, only three did so. The teams have therefore voted by eight to three that the arrangements are fair.

'I would suggest that the reason why F1 makes such good profits is not unassociated with the fact that Bernie – in my view – is a financial genius and that he works almost 24 hours a day in making the whole F1 business succeed.'

Looking to the longer term, Mosley originally saw no reason why Ecclestone should not capitalise his business on the international stock exchanges of the world. 'The FIA would welcome that,' he insisted, 'because it would mean that every detail of the finances of F1 would be out in the open and nobody could complain. It would be to the benefit of everyone.

'We [the sport] have been going through an entrepreneurial stage which is now almost finished. The final stage is the development of pay-TV and digital transmission, which is already coming. There will then be a classic management phase, at which point Bernie may decide to take his company public.'

Meanwhile, Bernie gets richer. In the year to March 1996 he drew Britain's largest pay packet of £54.9 million. He also hit the headlines in 1997 when it was revealed that he had made a payment of £1 million to the Labour Party, which won that year's General Election. That finished Bernie's efforts to retain a low profile and he was subjected to a barrage of media interest.

Not that he should worry. Since 1989 he is judged to have earned £142 million in salary and dividends from his various companies. If digital television takes off, he and his family trusts could be another £750 million richer. Nice work if you can get it!

Dramatic vista. Venues like
Monaco give Grand Prix racing its
exclusive cachet.

On the Move

F1 is a global sport which operates from Buenos Aires to Barcelona, from Silverstone to Suzuka, throughout the season. Yet if one looks at any Grand Prix paddock, the layout is essentially the same. The garages have to be to a certain, very high, specification, the transporters and motorhomes parked in a very specific order (for the European races) and – for those events taking place outside Europe – very detailed and complex shipping arrangements have to be made. So here we examine how all this evolved, how an individual team equips its transporters, how the motorhomes operate and how they are directed into their prescribed positions in the paddock.

The modern F1 paddock is more than simply a multi-million-dollar parking lot. It is the focal point of the Grand Prix weekend, the place at which you can detect the sport's very heartbeat. It is also a meeting place, entertainment centre and high-price bazaar. Along the 'boulevard' separating the transporters from the motorhomes, a trained eye can detect deals being done as drivers lurk indiscreetly talking to rival team owners.

Beautiful people? David Coulthard meets Liz Hurley and Hugh Grant at the 1998 Monaco Grand Prix.

It is trim, civilised and very tidy. No rubbish or litter can be seen and the tarmac underfoot gives a reassuring sense of permanence in line with Mr Ecclestone's requirements. It is also here that the massed ranks of photographers can click away at the celebrity guests who regularly turn up to drink in the narcotic atmosphere. King Juan Carlos of Spain, the likes of Sylvester Stallone, Ryan Giggs, Liz Hurley, Hugh Grant and Emma Noble, plus sprigs of the aristocracy, ex-Chancellors of the Exchequer, junior members of the British Royal Family – and even Tony Blair – all conspire to make a goodly mix during the course of the average season.

The organisation of the paddock itself is under the control of Ecclestone's F1 Administration personnel. Like a huge Chinese puzzle, steering all the articulated transporters and lavish motorhomes into position is rather akin to berthing a couple of dozen QE2s without the aid of tugs.

It also calls for considerable co-ordination with all concerned being given specific times to arrive and get in the right order in the queue to make certain that the transporters obtain the correct access for the right position behind the pit lane garages. There is a firm pecking order here with the teams lined up in the order in which they finished the previous year's World Championship. Thus Williams can claim pole position for 1998, but McLaren will almost certainly replace them in the prime pit lane site next season.

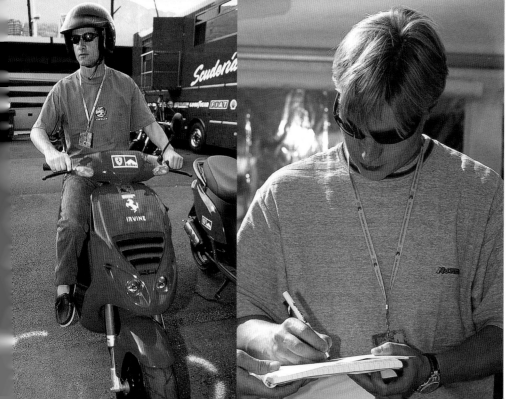

Above: Damon Hill leads Pedro Diniz – on and off the track, he would hope.

Far left: Ferrari driver Eddie Irvine scooters around the Monaco paddock. Good for keeping the fans at bay.

Left: Autograph time. Arrows driver Mika Salo makes time to oblige one of his fans.

SAUBER PETRONAS
Red Bull
Red Bull
ENERGY DRINK
PETRONAS MALAYSIA
GOODYEAR
GOODYEAR
PETRONAS
LD SEVEN

Paddock meetings. *Opposite:* Sauber driver Johnny Herbert shares a joke with Benetton team chief David Richards.

Above: Flavio Briatore *(left)* now heads the Supertec (previously Mecachrome) engine distribution operation. One of the highest-profile figures in F1, he previously ran the Benetton team. Here he talks to Ferrari technical director Ross Brawn.

Talking shop. Stewart-Ford technical director Alan Jenkins *(left)* chats to team driver Rubens Barrichello.

The heart of the business; F1's
paddock scene seldom varies.

For the 'fly-away' races, we investigate the complexities of packaging all the equipment for air travel, the rules governing transporting fuel by air, and how the cars are loaded up and delivered to the track at the other end of their journey.

The Benson & Hedges Jordan Mugen Honda team is a typical British-based F1 operation and its race director Trevor Foster took time off to explain the intricacies of the logistical challenge which faces the workforce every time the cars leave the factory *en route* to a race.

To every European Grand Prix the Jordan team takes two articulated transporters and a maximum-length (36 ft) fixed-wheelbase truck. One of the artics carries three F1 cars and all the spares, including a stand-by monocoque; the second trailer includes a meeting room for the engineers – effectively a portable office – while the rear section includes all the electrical equipment and a workshop area with a lathe, small milling machine and a welding machine.

'The fixed-wheelbase truck is purely a packhorse,' explains Foster. 'It carries all the garage equipment, all the banners, all the light pods, everything like that. It's just a storage wagon. There are also our two motorhomes plus another fixed-wheelbase truck which supports those two motorhomes, carrying all the tables, chairs, fridges, freezers, all the cooking facilities and the mobile cooking trailer.'

Main photo: The two Jordan Grand Prix transporters backed up against the pits contain everything needed to service the cars, while another transporter *(below)* becomes a hospitality area.

Spares for Every Occasion

In terms of car spares, Jordan plans to bring 'three sets of everything' plus what's on the car. In fact this amounts to three sets of spare bodywork, five sets of suspension components, around 70 sets of wheel rims and the refuelling rigs.

'To give you an indication, when we take all this equipment on "fly-away" races outside Europe, we take around 20,000 kilogrammes of kit,' says Foster. 'That means you are looking at 87 freight cases – what we call packhorses – of differing sizes, plus three cars as rolling chassis, of course.'

Transporting fuel is another matter altogether. Due to international airline regulations, it has to be transported in 50-litre drums in special aircraft, separate from those carrying the cars. All the F1 fuel suppliers get together and ship their products on a single aircraft to the races outside Europe. This 'hazardous load', which also includes the in-car and hand-held fire extinguishers and any aerosol products required, tends to be packaged up around a week ahead of the cars before being sent on its highly specialised way.

'Obviously, every component you take has to be listed,' explains Foster, 'and normally what happens is that at the start of the season we tend to change around 30 per cent of our packhorse boxes to accommodate the design details of the new car, because each is individually designed to carry three nose cones, ten sets of wheels, or whatever.

'This is of enormous benefit when you require a quick turn-round between races. Take the return from Monaco, for example: the transporters arrive at the factory around Tuesday lunchtime and the cars have to be ready and delivered to the airport for shipping to Montreal for the Canadian Grand Prix less than 48 hours later.

'This schedule is quite manageable, because as soon as we get back from Monaco, the components are just taken out of the transporters and put into pre-cleaned boxes all ready for despatch. These are not just boxes, remember, but specialist packing cases with drawers inside intended to take wishbones, uprights and gearboxes. So the whole process is methodical and very structured.

'Once the boxes are all packed, they are loaded into two "curtain sider" trucks which are used to transport the cars to the airport for the five or so fly-away races we have each season.'

In order to prevent the airport concerned having its traffic flow terminally clogged up by arriving and departing transporters, the teams are given a precise arrival slot for their trucks by the staff at Ecclestone's F1 Administration organisation, which organises the cargo flights.

'If you miss your slot, then you go to the back of the queue,' grins Foster. 'We supervise the off-loading and then each box is individually weighed. We get so much cargo allowed free as part of the FOCA rates, after which we get charged so much a kilogramme over that level. So obviously the packing is quite a crucial issue, because if you have a box which is too big, then you are just wasting volume needlessly. If you are not prudent with your packing, you suddenly find yourselves taking three or four boxes more than you could get away with. Our system keeps the cost well under control.'

The actual business of moving the cars from race to race is also considerably more structured and organised than it was, say, four decades ago. In the 1950s and early 1960s many so-called F1 transporters were little more than converted buses which overheated and simmered their arthritic way across gruelling Alpine passes in that pre-autoroute era.

Mechanics doubled as truck drivers and stayed at the wheel for as long as was necessary to get the job done. Driving through the night prior to preparing a Grand Prix car for practice was all part of the business, with no thought given to the potential damage which could be sustained – by both car and driver – as a consequence of errors made by a bleary-eyed workforce which had been without proper rest for more than 24 hours.

Inner sanctum. A place for everything and everything in its place.

The sharp end. With cars and
mechanics in the pits, the team set
about the task of qualifying.

Back in 1956 Bruce Halford, the Torquay hotelier who raced his own Maserati 250F in selected European Grands Prix, carried his car around Europe in an old 'Royal Blue' coach which had previously seen service between London and the West Country. The Connaught team – some assets of which would, ironically, eventually pass into Bernie Ecclestone's ownership after its closure in 1957 – similarly carried its valuable racing cars round in a fleet of rather disreputable-looking London buses.

The thought of a converted coach arriving at the gates of a contemporary F1 paddock in 1998 would be enough to throw Ecclestone – an obsessive control freak and perfectionist – into an apoplectic fit. The 'F1 Beverly HillBillies' image is as far from what he is looking for in the five-star, Blue Riband world of Grand Prix racing today as Jacques Villeneuve's latest haircut.

The two Jordan articulated Scania trucks weigh around 38 tons fully laden; the purpose-built trailers cost about £270,000 apiece. The 'tractors' are powered by 16-litre, straight-eight-cylinder engines developing 530 bhp; they are governed to the regulation 56 mph maximum, so the drivers use the clutch once to pull off, after which most functions are performed automatically.

'It almost does everything but steer itself,' says Foster. 'We estimate they will cover around 35,000 miles in a year – which isn't very much for a truck at all – and we usually change them about every two years. Of course, by then they're virtually as new, hardly run in. The guys who drive them love them like their own cars, cleaning and polishing them all the time, so there's almost a waiting list of people wanting to get their hands on them when they become available through the dealerships.

'With our test and race teams, Jordan now employs ten truck drivers,' he explains. 'Six on the race team, four on the test team. Returning from Barcelona, for example, the transporters would all be packed up on Sunday evening and the drivers would return to the paddock after a night's sleep in the hotel to make an early start around 6.30 a.m. the next morning.

'Of course, all the team truck drivers have to abide by the rigorous EU tachograph regulations and, to that end, each transporter has two drivers so that they are able to swap over and keep the rig running for the entire journey.

'The regulations are quite complicated, but generally it does mean that the transporters can get back to the Silverstone factory from most European destinations within a day and a half. Hungary is sometimes the exception with the transporter perhaps rolling in at ten o'clock Wednesday morning. But from most other places they are generally back by Tuesday lunchtime.'

Transporter investment: bespoke designs, replaced regularly.

chapter 2 THE CARS ARE ROLLING

Away from prying eyes; Williams mechanics pull one of the team's FW20s back into a pit lane garage.

One of the key aspects to be borne in mind during a Grand Prix weekend is the business of scrutineering the cars. This involves checks for rule conformity, safety and security and making sure that none of the teams has incorporated some sort of illegal control system – traction control, perhaps – which would give its drivers an unfair advantage.

The requirements of the scrutineers have progressed dramatically over the past 25 years. After Jochen Rindt's Lotus 72 won the 1970 British Grand Prix at Brands Hatch, there was a suspicion that its rear wing was higher than permitted. However, rather than being rolled straight into a secure scrutineering bay immediately after coming off the track, the victorious Lotus was taken on a victory lap mounted on the back of a trailer.

It was then delivered back to the scrutineers, by which time the wing was found to be legal. Legend has it that the mechanics sat very firmly on the wing during the victory lap, bending it back below the regulation height in preparation for its subsequent examination!

The rules also once permitted all fluid containers on the cars to be topped up to the level they were at before the race, prior to scrutineering. This inevitably opened the door to all sorts of fun and games with some teams re-filling oil catch tanks, for example, to the absolute brim in order to squeeze through the post-race checks in conformity with the minimum weight limit.

This rather loose interpretation of the technical regulations reached the height of absurdity in 1982 when the British-based FOCA-aligned teams were locked in a battle with the governing body over the legality of the new breed of 1.5-litre turbocharged engine which had been pioneered by Renault and Ferrari. The FOCA teams mainly used 3-litre Cosworth Ford DFV engines and many British engineers believed that the 1.5 litre supercharged regulation – which had been on the statute book for more than 15 years – did not permit exhaust-driven turbochargers. Renault and Ferrari, happy that they had more powerful engines to make up for their chassis design deficiencies, believed it did. So the British teams hit on a clever ruse.

With considerable ingenuity, Lotus, Williams, Brabham and the rest sought to drive a coach and horses through the meaning of the regulations, aiming to legitimise their efforts to race illegally by bending the interpretation of the rules. They were seeking to exploit a passage that defined a car's weight as 'the weight of the car in running order with its normal quantities of lubricants and coolants, but without any fuel or driver on board'.

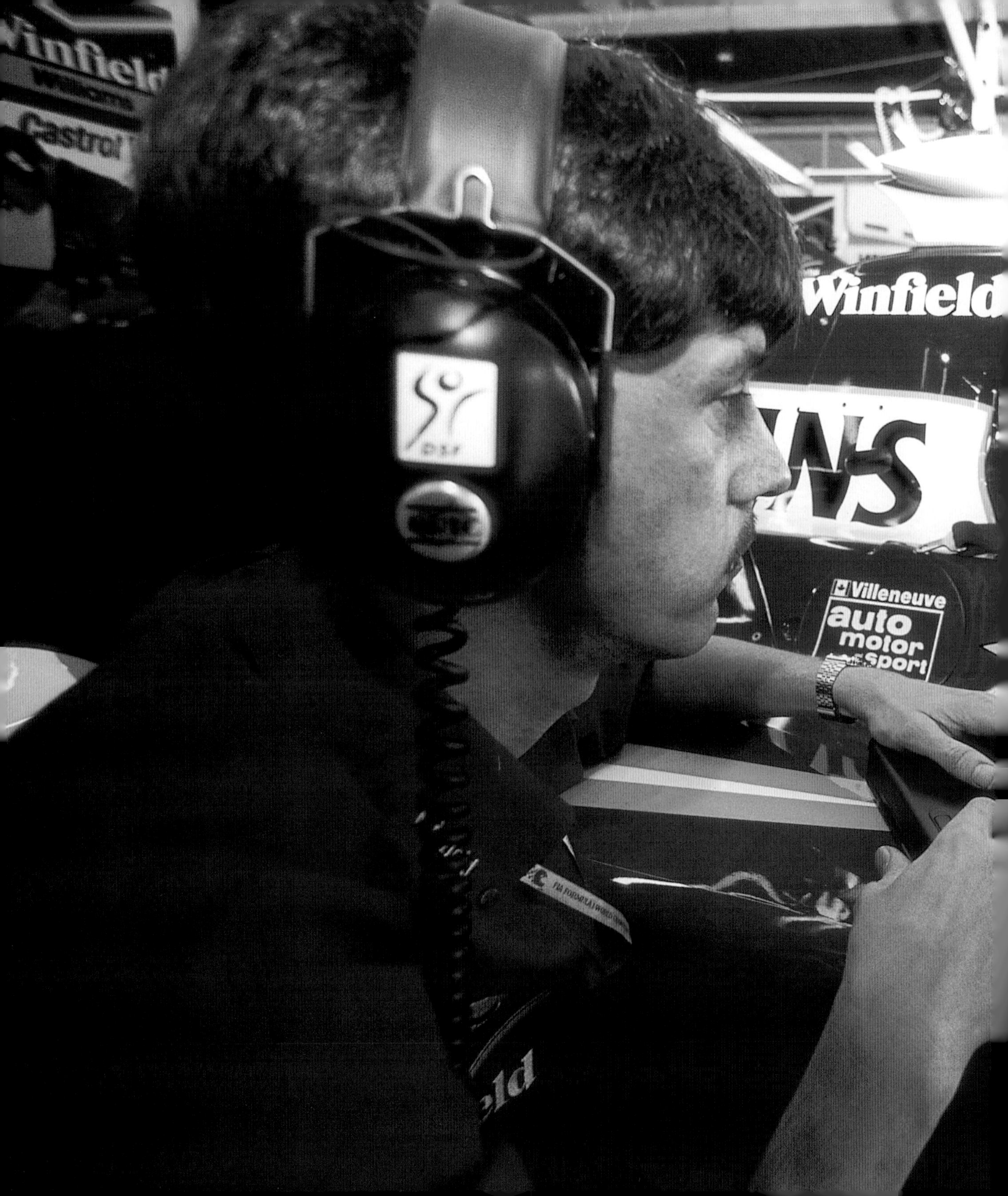
Winfield
Castrol
Winfield
Villeneuve
auto
motor
sport

THE CARS ARE ROLLING

A Williams engineer ponders the technical data.

The modern-day F1 driver's overalls almost drip with sponsorship identification – most of it from companies who invest in the team as a whole.

In line with the previous practice of topping up oil tanks to achieve the correct weight, the British teams now decided to run with water receptacles for brake cooling purposes. It was explained to gullible outsiders that jets of water were to be sprayed into the brake ducts, thereby reducing the temperature of the incoming air.

In fact, they were being disingenuous. The real idea was to jettison most of this water ballast early in the race, in the general direction of the brake ducts, race for the balance of the event below the prevailing 580 kg minimum weight limit and then, prior to scrutineering, top up the water tank to ensure that the car tipped the scales above the limit at the post-race check.

It was perhaps not surprising that Nelson Piquet's winning Brabham BT49C and Keke Rosberg's second-place Williams FW07C were disqualified from the 1982 Brazilian Grand Prix at Rio as a result of this scam. Renault, whose turbocharged machine had finished third on the road, lodged an official protest. This was rejected by the race stewards, but Renault then appealed to the FIA, which duly upheld their objection. The Renault won the race as a result.

It is a measure of the political turmoil which split Grand Prix racing asunder at that time that the issue of brake cooling was being used as a bargaining point by the FOCA teams as they battled, under Ecclestone's direction, to establish their claim to a share in the F1 television coverage rights.

The next race on the programme was the San Marino Grand Prix at Imola, which was boycotted by the FOCA-aligned teams on the basis that they 'could not design new cars for the new regulations in time'. Eventually order was re-established and Grand Prix racing settled down to thrive under the terms of the Concorde Agreement, this little hiccup over 'water bottles' notwithstanding.

Gradually, throughout the 1980s, rule implementation became ordered and codified. This applied to scrutineering procedures as much as anything else, yet even as late as 1992, when Gerhard Berger's winning McLaren-Honda came close to being disqualified from the Canadian Grand Prix, those inspecting the cars still had to take pot luck at many tracks when it came to locating a level 'flat patch' on which to complete crucial measuring procedures.

Berger had won the race in the McLaren MP4/7A only after Nigel Mansell's Williams FW14B had ploughed off the track as the Englishman pulled an ill-advised overtaking manoeuvre on Ayrton Senna's sister McLaren and the Brazilian had then retired with an electrical problem. It was only the second win of Berger's three-year tenure with McLaren and a success greeted with great pleasure by all his colleagues.

Yet a preliminary post-race inspection revealed the car's rear wing dimensions to be right on the outer margins of acceptability. In those days the FIA scrutineers had no precise weighing platform on which to check such dimensions and the car was examined at three different locations in the pit lane before being taken along to one of the garages where it was finally pronounced legal.

That episode was a distillation of precisely what Formula 1 engineering is all about. It involves studying and assimilating a detailed volume of rigorously specified regulations and exploiting them right up to the edge. The real challenge is to maximise the car's performance potential without attracting the unwanted attention of those ever-vigilant individuals, the FIA scrutineers.

Jacques Villeneuve in deep discussion with his engineer.

Complexity at work; the F1
steering wheel includes all manner
of secondary controls.

Policing the F1 Beat

McLaren chief Ron Dennis hit the nail firmly on the head when he commented: 'In Formula 1, the scrutineers are motor racing's equivalent of the Customs and Excise. During a race weekend they can come into your premises any time, as often as they want.'

The main difference, of course, is that most competing F1 teams are actually expecting the scrutineers to pay a visit more often than the Customs and Excise. On the other hand, no matter how even-handed the governing body attempts to be, there is an inevitable tang of thinly suppressed competition between the teams and the scrutineers.

It is certainly hoped that nobody goes out of their way deliberately to transgress the rules, but in the feverishly competitive F1 environment it is normal to push things to the edge. This has caught several teams out over the years, but one of the most embarrassing episodes of all came in the 1985 San Marino Grand Prix at Imola.

Alain Prost's McLaren MP4/2B-TAG had won the race commandingly after an early battle with

Opposite: David Coulthard keeps a close track on his rivals' practice times before heading out for another qualifying stint. Then it is the turn of the pit crew *(above)* to watch the monitor intently before their driver's return and the inevitable set-up changes to come.

The scrutineering bay provides the teams with the facilities to measure their cars in minute detail in order to check that they conform with the F1 technical regulations. Best to be sure; you never quite know when the next random check will take place.

Ayrton Senna's Lotus-Renault, but when the victorious machine was pushed onto the scales, it turned out to be a couple of kilogrammes below the minimum weight limit. Checking and re-checking could not alter this painful reality, so Prost and McLaren were disqualified from the race and victory was inherited by Lotus driver Elio de Angelis.

In situations like this, a finely judged call fell just the wrong side of the penalty line. Prior to the race the McLaren engineers were obliged to guess how much ballast would be needed on Alain's car, taking into account the fuel load and its consumption rate, and wear on brake pads and tyres. It was just one of those things.

Keeping to the Rules

Nowadays there is a strict scrutineering routine which is carried out with meticulous regularity throughout the F1 World Championship season. It begins on the Thursday afternoon prior to each individual race when a posse of FIA officials arrives at each garage in turn for the first of many inspections of a team's competing cars.

Before any car can even be allowed out on the circuit for a single lap, it has to be scrutineered in detail by officials from the sport's governing body to make sure it complies with all the exhaustive F1 safety regulations. This is part of an on-going procedure that continues throughout every Grand Prix weekend which ensures that every competing car strictly conforms with every aspect of the rules every second it is on the track during practice, qualifying and the race.

The scrutineers, who answer to Charlie Whiting, the head of the FIA's Technical Department, and the Technical Delegate, Jo Bauer, start by checking every single item which may have an influence on the car's safety and security - even though

the governing body has already given the green light to individual car designs by the imposition of pre-season crash testing of the chassis. The FIA team checks that the cars' nose sections have not been modified and that the rear impact structures remain the same, then moves on to examine the fuel filler, seat belts and fire extinguishers, and ensure that the cockpit head rests are the right size.

There is, of course, little to be gained at this point in the weekend from measuring the cars for dimensional conformity. It is a matter of no consequence whatsoever if the FIA officials should find a rear wing, for example, which is slightly too high. But by the same token all the competing teams voluntarily submit their cars to detailed checks during the course of the weekend.

During the course of Saturday morning, a queue of cars will be pushed up the pit lane to the official scrutineering bay to be checked over prior to official qualifying. The cars are rolled onto a highly sophisticated weighing platform to ensure they conform with the 600 kg minimum weight limit, while a flat surface is raised beneath the car to make contact with the 'reference plane' from which all the height measurements are calculated.

As far as the engines are concerned, only occasionally does the FIA take the opportunity of checking the bore/stroke dimensions to ensure that they conform with the current 3-litre capacity limit. In the past the FIA staff have examined the bores with a specially designed feeler gauge which could be inserted through the spark plug aperture.

Instead, perhaps three or four times each season, the scrutineers will randomly select an engine to be stripped down for detailed examination. This is not treatment which any particular team feels it is being singled out for, and all would comply with any such requirement instantly should the request be made.

Random Checks

Of course, once practice and qualifying get under way, all the teams and drivers remain mindful of the fact that their progress could be the subject of the various random checks initiated by the scrutineers. These include fuel sampling, when specimens of the fuel will be taken and subjected to a gas chromatograph test, the results of which are then checked against the 'fingerprint' of the fuel sample lodged with the FIA prior to each individual race.

The FIA takes a similarly stringent attitude towards the checking of the sophisticated electronic software systems which are part and parcel of every contemporary Grand Prix car. After concerns that the governing body lacked the detailed technology to check these systems in years past, it has more recently evolved more comprehensive and wide-ranging methods of policing this complicated area.

This is done by pre-approving specific versions of software submitted by the teams. These are checked at source code level to ensure that they cannot carry out any function which the scrutineers might feel they should not – illegal traction control, for example – and a copy is duly taken.

Thereafter, at any time over the race weekend, the FIA personnel can descend on any car in the pit lane and request that the software be uploaded onto their own computer where it is checked byte for byte with the reference copy lodged earlier. This takes only about five minutes, even though such random testing might cause a crucial interruption to the team's technical set-up programme during the course of any particular session.

'On Friday at Montreal in '98 we had an example of one of the FIA scrutineers arriving in our garage asking to upload the details of our software for a routine check,' recalled McLaren engineer Steve Hallam. 'Our initial reaction, quite naturally I suppose, was, "Oh no, not in the middle of a

The minutiae of pit lane life; checking brake temperatures is all part of the complex technical package.

practice session," and, to be fair, he agreed to wait until the cars had stopped running before he did so, although he insisted on remaining in the garage until then. Of course, this is quite within the scrutineers' rights and it is inevitable that when your car is competitive you expect it to be checked pretty frequently, which of course proves to be the case.

'The scrutineering bay is open from 7.30 in the morning until 7.30 in the evening over the days of a Grand Prix, during which time you can satisfy yourself at any time that your car conforms to the rules simply by pushing it down there and using the FIA equipment. When 7.30 in the evening arrives, they place a marker cone behind the last car remaining in the queue and if anybody else subsequently turns up, they find themselves placed at the head of the queue when the bay opens for business the following morning.

'But Ron is quite right. It *is* a bit like the Customs and Excise. Right down to the onus being on us as team entrants to prove our cars' conformity to the regulations rather than the other way around!'

Another possible interruption comes in the form of the pit lane weight check. An FIA computer has a 'random generator' in the programme and, on average, selects about one in four of the cars which arrive in the pit lane. The computer may say 'weigh the third car to come in', which makes the whole process beyond suspicion, because obviously nobody knows which is going to be the third car to enter the pit lane at any one moment during a practice or qualifying session.

The net result of this, of course, is that sometimes a car and driver can go three races without being checked. Yet, on the other hand, it is possible that one car could be checked on three occasions during an hour-long qualifying session. Small wonder the drivers approach the pit lane entrance with more than a passing degree of fear and trepidation.

A Scrutineering Record

The FIA stewards retain detailed records of the checks carried out and each check the scrutineers have made over the course of a Grand Prix weekend. As an example, on 7 June 1998, the day of the Canadian Grand Prix at Montreal's Circuit Gilles Villeneuve, Technical Delegate Jo Bauer oversaw the following examinations.

After the warm-up, a fuel sample was taken from Olivier Panis's Prost-Peugeot. Before the race began, fuel samples were taken from Jacques Villeneuve's Williams FW20 and Johnny Herbert's Sauber C17 and these were duly processed and analysed during the course of the event.

In addition, the thickness of the brake discs on all cars was checked, software checks were carried out on Jarno Trulli's Prost-Peugeot and, when the field was on the grid, it was checked that all cars had their tyres properly fitted by the time the five minute signal was given.

After the race the scrutineers weighed Villeneuve's Williams, the Ferrari F300s of Michael Schumacher and Eddie Irvine (first- and third-place finishers), the Benetton B198s of Giancarlo Fisichella and Alexander Wurz (second and fourth) and the Stewart-Fords of Rubens Barrichello and Jan Magnussen (fifth and sixth), plus Pedro Diniz's Arrows A19, Ricardo Rosset's Tyrrell 026 and the Minardi M198 of Shinji Nakano.

In addition, the top six finishers were examined for front and rear wing height/overhang, front and rear wing width, side pod height, rear winglet height, bodywork around the front wheels, overall bodywork height and width, skid block thickness and rear wing configuration.

Schumacher's Ferrari and Magnussen's Stewart also had fuel samples taken. These, together with Villeneuve's, were found to be in accordance with the rules – as indeed were all other elements of the cars checked. The race results could therefore be confirmed.

Mercedes motor sport manager
Norbert Haug (left) with
McLaren MD Ron Dennis: the men
behind the partnership which
produced the dominant 1998
McLaren MP4/13-Mercedes.

Confidential Clarification

The FIA Technical Department does not merely confine itself to the business of scrutineering cars at the races, or implementing the rules as it feels it should. There is also a far more delicate and diplomatic challenge involved when it comes to administering the business of technical queries from individual teams.

The system devised is intended to protect the technical initiatives of individual competitors. Unfortunately certain events in 1997 and '98 caused some critics to suggest that this mechanism creates a loophole by which the governing body can overrule and undermine the position of the Technical Department.

It is, however, crucial to understand how the mechanism works for it certainly acknowledges that the essence of F1 competition is stealing a march over one's rivals. If a team has a novel technical development, it sends a formal inquiry to the FIA Technical Department asking for a clarification as to whether it believes such a system is permissible under the existing rules. The FIA Technical Delegate considers the matter and then sends his considered reply. But only to that team. To circulate all rivals would be to unfairly negate any advantage the inquiring team had achieved through its own ingenuity.

At the 1997 British Grand Prix the FIA issued a rule clarification to the McLaren team relating to an inquiry over the controls for F1 electronic throttle systems. This enabled engine revs to be used as an additional control parameter in an effort to smooth out the engine's torque characteristics. The governing body denied that it had opened the door to banned traction control systems 'by any other name' by pointing out that the system did not involve response from any wheel sensors and was not therefore a 'closed loop' mechanism, which would have been illegal.

That said, it was not clear whether McLaren lodged its inquiry purely for its own purposes – or had perhaps second-guessed what a rival team was doing and wanted an indication as to whether it should follow that route. Not that the reason for the inquiry would be any concern of the FIA's. It would simply send its reply and that would be the end of the matter.

The Stewards Decide Differently

At around the same time, McLaren also sent a request for clarification as to whether its clever asymmetrical braking system – which retarded the outside rear wheel less than the inside one in an effort to stabilise the car in certain types of corner – was legal. This system was controlled by a second brake pedal and Whiting sent a response confirming his belief that the system, as explained by McLaren, conformed to the rules.

However, Ferrari thought otherwise and, at the Brazilian Grand Prix at the start of 1998, lodged a protest. On this occasion, the braking system, by now developed for Williams and Jordan in addition to McLaren, was declared illegal by the stewards.

Despite the fact that McLaren had consulted Whiting on every aspect of this secondary braking system, stewards Nazir Hoosein, Radovan Novak and Elcio de Sao Thiago chose to ignore his viewpoint and decided that the systems should be outlawed with immediate effect. The main thrust of the

Mika Häkkinen and his McLaren were the subject of a protest in Brazil over the car's asymmetrical braking system.

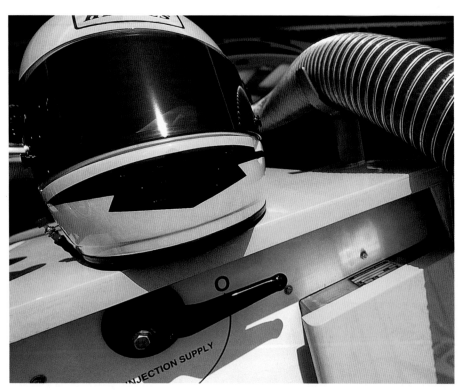

The fuel the teams use must match a sample lodged with the FIA before the meeting and random checks are carried out to ensure that it does.

Ferrari team's objection centred on a raft of possible breaches of the technical rules. In an effort to encompass every possible area of infringement, the Italian team claimed that the three rival teams did not comply with 'one or more' of the rules concerning the prohibition of four-wheel steering, anti-lock and power brakes, traction control and lack of a brake system which has at least two separate systems operated by the same pedal.

It was eventually decided that the principal function of the system was steering rather than braking, with the result that the systems were prohibited from that point onwards.

'While we must commend McLaren, Williams and Jordan for keeping the FIA Technical Department informed and seeking their opinion,' said an official bulletin, 'the stewards must state with respect that, at the same time, this has not constituted a cast-iron defence as the stewards are not bound to concur with the opinions expressed by the FIA Technical Department.'

However, Ferrari dramatically overstepped the bounds of propriety by suggesting that the cars under protest infringed Article 2.3 of the rules relating to the stewards of the meeting's right to 'exclude a vehicle whose construction is deemed to be dangerous'.

The stewards censured the Italian team 'for bringing up an issue of dangerous construction especially when Mr Charlie Whiting specifically stated that this is not the case. McLaren, Williams and Jordan are very responsible competitors and such inferences are not warranted.'

From this example, it would be all too easy to conclude that the implementation of F1's rules and regulations requires major revision. The feeling among some teams is that the rotation of stewards from race to race inevitably produces a lack of consistency in the decision-making process. FIA President Max Mosley, on the other hand, feels that sufficient debate takes place between the various groups of stewards during the course of a season to ensure that a reasonable balance is sustained.

The question of whether the authority of the FIA's Technical Department was undermined by the decision of the stewards at the 1998 Brazilian Grand Prix is not regarded as a long-term problem. The FIA's view is that the very fact that the stewards contradicted the Technical Department shows their independence of purpose.

Less charitable voices suggest that there is an alternative conclusion to be reached: namely that the FIA can influence the stewards to reach conclusions of which they approve. Such contentions are rejected by the governing body, which claims the whole structure is designed to ensure objective consideration of any issue and dispassionate application of penalties.

Producing the Yellow Card

Once the race meeting gets under way the race director is keeping a watchful eye out for a variety of rule transgressions. In the interests of safety the pit lane is subject to a strict speed limit and exceeding this usually results in a modest fine during practice or qualifying, but a ten-second 'stop-go' penalty is imposed for an infringement during the race.

This involves the offending driver coming in to stop at his own pit for ten seconds and then accelerating back into the race. During such a penalty stop the competitor is not permitted the unfair advantage of refuelling or changing tyres, so incurring such a delay can mean a second or third pit stop for the guilty party. The 'stop-go' method is generally regarded as a satisfactory system of instant justice which ensures that the competitor is penalised without the time-consuming prospect of a row after the race which delays the confirmation of the results.

In the case of dangerous driving, the stewards will deliberate at length before imposing a penalty. Disqualification is a possibility, in which case the race results may remain provisional until an appeal is considered. If this is rejected then a further appeal can go to the FIA World Council, which will review the situation and have the final say.

However, history tells us that proceeding with an appeal tends to be a fruitless task. Best to take your medicine on the day, as the FIA has been known to increase penalties, both financial and in terms of race suspensions, for those who don't know when it is prudent to stop arguing.

Michael Schumacher waits for the signal to rejoin the race as he serves a ten-second stop-go penalty in the Ferrari pit.

chapter 3 BEHIND THE SCENES

This chapter examines a team's operational structures throughout a Grand Prix weekend, considering matters such as paddock procedure, the format of practice and qualifying, tyre choice, timing systems, the teams' catering arrangements and the build-up of tension during the count-down to the start of the race. We also take a look at the role of the safety car, the special demands of racing in the wet, the structure of a leading team and the rivalry that inevitably exists between the two groups of engineers and mechanics tending each of the two drivers' cars, before turning our attention to the crucial role played by pit-stop strategy and the meticulously synchronised team work that forms the basis of an efficient refuelling stop.

The Weekend's Programme

Monza or Magny-Cours, Silverstone or Suzuka, the format of the Grand Prix weekend follows the same rigid pattern the world over. Gone are the days when individual race organisers had the right to frame their own practice schedules, and the streets of Monte Carlo echoed to F1 exhaust notes from as early as seven o'clock in the morning.

The fixed schedule imposes a disciplined format on the weekend, although Monaco continues to be permitted its own individuality with the first day's practice taking place on Thursday rather than Friday. This is a ploy which enables the Principality and the surrounding French Riviera to earn extra income from the fans and holidaymakers who always swarm into the area for that memorable, spectacular and very special weekend in May.

Enter most F1 paddocks on Friday morning at around 8.00 a.m. and you could be forgiven for thinking that life on Earth had ended. Only a handful of hardy souls have made their way through the computerised pass control which enables the FIA to monitor precisely who has arrived at the paddock and at what time they came through the entry turnstiles.

Di Spires provides a traditional English breakfast for journalists at the Ford motorhome before the start of the day's proceedings.

The motorhome brigade is, of course, already hard at it cooking breakfast and the mechanics, most of whose preparation work on the cars has been carried out the previous day, will be fed and ready for action by about 9.00 a.m., still two hours before the first car is due to edge out onto the circuit.

In the past most of the team members tended to arrive at the races on Thursday, but the added complexity of the pit lane garage set-up, with banks of computers for the on-car telemetry systems, now means that at least some of the crew has to arrive on Wednesday as the amount of work involved in 'dressing' the garage simply could not be completed with a Thursday arrival.

Above: Bridgestone offers lunch to many of the paddock regulars.

Right: Media shuttles transport photographers and journalists around the track throughout the weekend.

Opposite, top: Journalists benefit from state-of-the-art press facilities situated over the pit complex. Photographers *(opposite, bottom)* are also catered for with provision being made for film processing and the wiring of photos around the world.

Practice and Qualifying

Practice and qualifying at Grands Prix follows an absolutely rigorous schedule with free practice on Friday taking place from 11.00 to 12 noon and then again from 13.00 to 14.00. On Saturday there is another session from 9.00 to 11.00, split up by a half-hour interval from 9.45 to 10.15 which enables any cars that have broken down on the circuit to be returned to the paddock.

The really crucial pre-race session is the hour-long qualifying stint from 13.00 to 14.00 on Saturday, during which each competitor is allowed a maximum of 12 laps in which to set his time. The tempo of practice is quite muted on Friday morning with the circuit sometimes remaining devoid of cars for the first half-hour or so as everybody waits for somebody else to go out and effectively clean up the dust from the racing line.

Once the cars get into the swing of things Fridays are often spent working out race set-ups for Sunday, so with cars running on a mix of full and empty fuel tanks it is difficult to be certain who is doing precisely what. On Saturday morning the whole pace of the weekend picks up and one begins to get a clearer indication of possible race form.

Throughout Friday and Saturday morning the teams will have been experimenting with the different tyre compounds available to them. With a vigorous tyre war being fought out in 1998 between Bridgestone and Goodyear, each manufacturer turned up with a 'prime' tyre compound (the one they judge their runners will need) and a back-up 'option' compound which is on hand 'just in case'.

Ten sets of dry-weather tyres are allowed during the course of the race weekend for each car, plus seven sets of wets, which must include no more than three different types. However, by Saturday

Opposite: Drivers' eye views: a battery of cameras awaits the annual team photograph *(top)*, and the view from the startline at Magny-Cours.

Below: Bridgestone tyres at the ready for F1 action with Benetton.

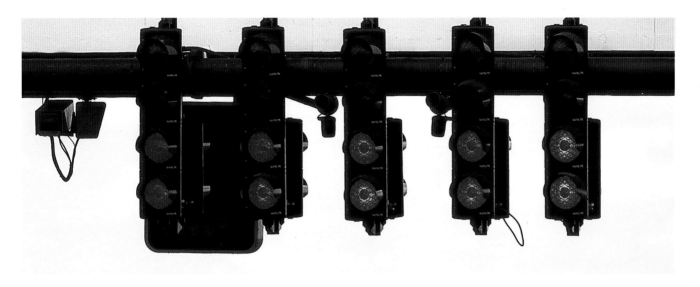

lunchtime – before qualifying – each driver must make his choice of tyre compound, after which he is committed to using it for the rest of the weekend. A maximum of seven sets of tyres can be used through qualifying and the following day's race.

After qualifying the fastest three drivers have to attend a mandatory press conference in the media centre before being allowed to return to the peace of their motorhomes to carry out the technical debrief with their engineers. They will probably then have a light snack, and possibly a work-out or some physiotherapy, and then return to their hotels for a light meal and an early night.

Sunday morning produces a steady build-up of pressure on drivers, mechanics and engineers. Four and a half hours before the scheduled start of the race there is a 30-minute final warm-up session during which the car's race set-up is checked out and final decisions are taken on refuelling strategy. Refuelling was re-introduced from the start of 1994, largely to add to the spectacle, and races tend to be won or lost in the pit lane as a result rather than out on the circuit.

At 11.00 a.m. on race morning comes the drivers' briefing. Attendance is mandatory and heavy fines can be inflicted on anyone who should miss it, or even be late. In reality, there is little chance of that, since each team has one member deputed to make sure that the competitors are on parade at the right moment.

With about 40 minutes to go before the start of the race, the drivers begin to prepare for action. The pit lane exit opens with half an hour to go, at which point they complete at least one warm-up lap before taking their places on the grid.

The starting gantry over the pits straight has five large red lights which are extinguished one at a time at one-minute intervals in the final count-down prior to the formation lap. With one minute to go, the engines are fired up and the grid is cleared before the field accelerates away, holding station behind the pole position car. At the end of the lap, the drivers pause briefly on the grid, waiting for the race director to give the starting signal. The five lights go on one by one; when all five are extinguished the start is on. This is the point of no return beyond which the engineers and mechanics can have precious little effect on the outcome of the race.

In a deafening wall of sound, the pack is left to accelerate ferociously towards the first corner, jostling madly for position in what seems like a choking cloud of dust. From this point on the pit

Above: The gantry housing the five red lights facing the starting grid. When they are extinguished, the race is on.

Opposite, top: Jacques Villeneuve rides round the circuit during the pre-race drivers' parade lap, one of the few occasions when the paying public can see their heroes minus their helmets.

Opposite, bottom: The World Champion in his car on the grid, ready to go about his work.

Overleaf: The pack speed away on the opening lap of the Canadian Grand Prix. With so many closely matched cars fighting for position, first-lap collisions are commonplace.

crew can simply keep its fingers firmly crossed and hopefully monitor the proceedings. Their job is now done and, from here on, everything rests on the drivers until the first refuelling stop.

All this, of course, assumes there is no first-corner accident. At the 1998 Canadian Grand Prix the race was red-flagged to a halt only seconds after the start when Alexander Wurz's Benetton somersaulted into the run-off area over the top of Jean Alesi's Sauber. The cars were stopped and, since the race had not yet been running for two laps, it was restarted over the full distance.

When the restarted race was again disrupted by a first-corner shunt, the safety car was employed to slow the field and keep the contest running at reduced speed. This involves the pack forming up behind a specially prepared 5.4-litre, V8-engined, 400 bhp AMG Mercedes CLK driven by former British F3 Champion Oliver Gavin, who is retained by the FIA to carry out this function at all rounds of the F1 World Championship. The essence of the safety car's success is that it is capable of running quickly enough not to frustrate the F1 drivers running at reduced speed behind it. As an indication of the CLK's potential – and Gavin's ability – when the safety car was deployed at the start of the rain-soaked 1997 Belgian Grand Prix, the Englishman led the pack round Spa-Francorchamps averaging just under 80 mph. On a treacherously slippery circuit!

Opposite: Sometimes that first corner can go badly wrong. Alexander Wurz's Benetton finally landed in the gravel, minus its front wheels. Before Wurz abandons his shattered car, he remembers that the rules require him to refit the steering wheel – irrespective of whether the front wheels are there or not!

Below: The Mercedes safety car, fast enough to keep the pack running at a respectable speed during danger periods of the race.

Split-seconds Make the Difference

Since 1992 McLaren's associate company TAG Heuer has been responsible for the timing systems at every round of the FIA Formula 1 World Championship. It is a task which involves a 20-strong team spending much of the week prior to an individual race setting up the screens and radio antennae which will allow every lap of practice, qualifying and the race to be timed precisely to three decimal places.

The system relies on a small electronic transponder fitted to each competing car. This transmits information on each car's speed and lap times at the finish line and at two intermediate points round the lap. This is beamed to a central computer which then collates the data and displays it on screen, not only in the pit lane but also in the media centre and on any information screens which may be situated around the track.

With straightline speeds, elapsed time through the three sectors of a lap, time spent at refuelling stops and maximum speeds all provided, the TAG Heuer system represents an invaluable tool in the quest to analyse and improve Grand Prix car performance throughout the field.

Opposite: Jacques Villeneuve takes a chance to see how his times are shaping up on one of the TAG Heuer portable screens.

Below: Giancarlo Fisichella at speed in the Benetton B198. The transponder on the car sends his lap time to the pits, enabling other drivers to gauge their competitiveness.

Feeding the Workers

Like an army, of course, F1 crews tend to march on their stomachs. Williams has its own contracted catering company run by long-time fan and amateur hillclimb competitor Paul Edwards, and all other F1 teams have their own catering staff offering fare of correspondingly and consistently high standards along the length of the paddock.

While the action takes place on the circuit, Paul and his staff of two are busy rustling up on-circuit breakfasts for the mechanics in addition to VIP lunches and dinners for influential sponsors and business partners of the team, many of whom attend one or more races during the course of the season.

Edwards and his colleagues tend to purchase their supplies locally, although certain staple ingredients – 'like bacon, black pudding and thick-cut Oxford marmalade!' – are shipped out from Britain with the team. Over the course of three days, the Williams catering department can serve up to 1500 meals, so Paul's crew are under as much pressure in their own way as the race team mechanics.

Left: 'Petit France'. The Prost hospitality area is a popular meeting place for the media.

Below: Refuge: the Winfield motorhome provides well-earned seclusion for many drivers in the F1 paddock.

Team Work

Study in concentration: the McLaren-Mercedes squad on the pit wall, monitoring their cars' progress.

Team strategy is another crucial element which contributes to the successful running of a race. Some teams like Ferrari have a nominated number one driver (Michael Schumacher, in the case of the Italian team) and base their strategies on a supporting and subservient role for the number two driver.

Others, such as Williams and McLaren, apply generally equal treatment to their drivers in all but the most exceptional circumstances. An example of this even-handedness could be seen across the final four races of the 1996 F1 World Championship season when Williams team-mates Damon Hill and Jacques Villeneuve had the battle for the title crown exclusively to themselves.

The fact that they were allowed to compete against each other through to the final race of the season stood as a significant testimony to the effort expended by the Williams-Renault team in general – and the engineering staff under the direction of Patrick Head and Adrian Newey in particular.

After a quarter-century in the business, Head still remains as committed to F1 engineering excellence as ever. And, although he would not admit it freely, it is an open secret within Williams that Patrick believes that aiming for engineering excellence is the only way to sustain a team's competitive edge.

Results, in his view, flow directly from this crucial baseline. In this respect he and Frank Williams believe that the key to F1 success is not primarily linked to drivers. Buying the best driver and then furnishing him with a sub-standard car, hoping that he will somehow make the difference, is not their way. They aim to build the best cars on the basis that this, in itself, will attract the best drivers into their stable.

With no team orders to constrain the drivers' performance, the outcome of the 1996 World Championship contest now depended on two key factors: the rivals' own resilience under pressure and the legendary ability of the Williams team to field two cars of absolute competitive parity.

Yet behind the scenes at Williams lurks a well-honed sense of professional rivalry between the two separate sets of engineers and mechanics responsible for the preparation and operation of the two drivers' cars. While the mental attitude is very definitely 'Williams against the rest of the world' when it comes to the individual races, personal pride and a wish to see 'their' particular driver excel remains a significant motivating factor in the team's operation.

'The rivalry is well controlled inasmuch as it is the job of the mechanics to prepare the cars to the absolute best of their abilities,' agrees Patrick Head. 'Also, if they find something wrong on an individual car, they are duty bound to report it to the engineers – there are no individual "tweaks" developed by certain mechanics for one or other of the cars.

Waiting for the action. Olivier Panis with his back to the camera while team chief Alain Prost *(right)* daren't look at the timing screens on the pit wall.

Great partnership: Frank Williams (*right*) and his technical director Patrick Head.

'Yet there is an element of competition between the two sets of mechanics and engineers, and quite rightly a certain pride, involved here. When their car wins then it's obvious that they derive more pleasure, perhaps, than if the other car beats them. But this rivalry is strictly controlled within the overall team strategy.'

As in all Grand Prix teams, Williams has a well-defined technical and management structure which governs the way in which a race weekend takes shape from the very moment that the cars roll out of the transporters and line up in the pit lane garages early on a Thursday morning prior to a Grand Prix.

While team manager Dickie Stanford concentrates on sporting, administrative and logistical matters, the Williams technical operation is the responsibility of either technical director Patrick Head or operations manager James Robinson, these two key players making all the major decisions concerning the intricacies of chassis set-up and aerodynamic adjustments.

This sense of co-operation extended to relations between the two drivers, although both Hill and

Villeneuve demonstrates his own inimitable style as he heads across the paddock.

Villeneuve had their own well-defined preferences in terms of chassis set-up. Damon was enormously experienced in this area, having worked with the team ever since 1991 when he first took over the role of test driver before being promoted to the full-time race team two years later.

Villeneuve was much less experienced in the ways of F1 car set-up and arrived in the team that season with his own very specific ideas on the subject.

'He is still pursuing a rather different route,' said Head, 'but I think we've got to go with it on the basis that, if he's right, then it'll be an education for us, and if it's wrong then at least we will sort it out.

'Jacques says the way he sets up his car is not necessarily his style, but it is the only way he can drive our car and get good lap times out of it.'

The manner in which Villeneuve came to grips with the business of learning circuits which were totally new to him greatly impressed Adrian Newey, then the Williams team's chief designer prior to his switch to McLaren in 1997.

'In many ways he reminded me of Alain Prost in terms of his approach,' he notes approvingly. 'He does just enough to get the job done. He is good at conserving both himself and the equipment.'

The Pressure of the Race

Once the race begins, intra-team rivalries tend to be submerged beneath the greater good of the overall team performance. Both groups of mechanics get stuck in to refuel and change tyres on the cars as required.

It is a matter of pride among the mechanics and engineers that everybody performs as slickly and professionally as possible in the heat of battle, although minor setbacks such as problems with the refuelling rig not delivering its precise allocation of fuel into the car's tank, or a sticking wheel nut, can sometimes intervene to frustrate even the best-disciplined operation.

'The individual race engineers are also in charge in the sense that they operate elements such as refuelling strategy during the course of the race,' explains Head.

'No matter how carefully you may plan out what you think is the right race strategy it's always necessary to have a "What happens if he messes up the start?" Plan B available. But ultimately everybody works together on race day. The mechanics and engineers are all highly professional people and any suggestion that they might bog up one of the cars' refuelling stops, for example, to give their man an advantage is utterly ludicrous.'

Trackside advertising is another lucrative source of income for the F1 business.

Slippery When Wet

Racing in the rain is an ever-present hazard to be taken in one's stride by any Grand Prix driver. Yet while some drivers obviously worry about the challenge, others relish the opportunity to display their skills in conditions in which they know that many of their rivals are tempted to lift their right foot off the throttle pedal.

Damon Hill, for one, certainly isn't bothered about wet races. 'Obviously the visibility can be quite a problem,' he explains, 'but I'm not unduly concerned about racing in the rain. In fact, I pride myself on being quite good in the wet as I think I proved when I won in Japan in 1994 and again in Brazil in 1996. It evens things up, makes you concentrate harder than ever and can be pretty stimulating.'

One driver who knows more than most about the intricacies of racing in the wet is Jackie Stewart, the triple World Champion who retired from driving in 1973. Now 59, Stewart won the 1968 German Grand Prix at the Nürburgring in conditions of driving rain, low cloud and mist which were probably as bad as anything seen since.

'Wet-weather driving requires a rare delicacy of touch,' he explains, 'although sometimes it is possible to see a "car control" merchant really shining in the wet, generally on slow circuits.

'Obviously, you have to apply the power very much more progressively and that, in a way, helps teach you to become a better driver. There are two or three things you've got to avoid: really late braking is one. You can lock up the wheels and you don't have the room to sort out the situation as you do in the dry. You also use less road in the rain and, to get the best out of the situation, you need a very much softer-sprung car.'

Of course, one man who knew little about racing in the rain prior to the 1996 season was new Williams recruit Jacques Villeneuve. He had only ever raced in the rain on two previous occasions in his entire career prior to that year's Brazilian GP at Interlagos.

'I spun off there simply through inexperience,' he shrugged. 'But it didn't really take too long to get used to racing in the rain. You just have to treat all the controls with a lot more delicacy and consideration!'

Eddie Irvine treads carefully in his Ferrari as he pulls away from the Minardi of Esteban Tuero.

Anatomy of a Refuelling Stop

Most top Grand Prix teams spend many hours on empty test tracks honing their pit stop technique to near-perfection so that their drivers can benefit from the slickly choreographed performance – F1's equivalent of synchronised swimming.

The timing and planning of refuelling stops is just as important as carrying out the mechanics of the stop as near-perfectly as possible. Judging when a pit stop should be made involves balancing the all-up weight of a car with the amount of fuel necessary to cover the planned distance while at the same time taking into account tyre wear considerations.

Changes in track temperature may adversely affect tyre performance, which can cause a handling imbalance. If this is reported over the radio link by the driver, changes in pressure may have to be made to those tyres waiting to be fitted to the car at the next refuelling stop.

All competitors have a refuelling 'window' – a handful of laps during which they can make a scheduled refuelling stop. This is worked into the game plan to give the driver a degree of flexibility, possibly to take advantage of a close rival pitting earlier and enabling the other car to

The tension of a refuelling stop. The Williams crew is ready and waiting for Villeneuve.

stay out slightly longer in the hope of gaining a fractional track advantage before making its own stop.

On the other hand, if a car gets stuck in slow traffic – or looks as though it is closing onto the tail of back-markers quite quickly – it may be the best choice to bring that car in slightly early. Maximising the possibilities offered by this game of cat and mouse enacted between the finely matched front-runners can be of crucial importance in determining the outcome of the race. Top teams use specialised computer programmes with which to reassess fuel loads using the car's telemetry systems and these calculations can be performed in the time that it takes for the driver to complete a single lap.

Finally the decision is made and the car concerned comes into view in the pit lane. The driver has to have his wits about him at this stage in the race, for not only must he remember to engage his car's pit lane speed limiter, he also has to concentrate on making the swiftest and most accurate approach to his pit, stopping precisely adjacent to the mechanics who are waiting with the four replacement tyres.

As the Canadian rolls to a halt, mechanics fall on the car in precisely drilled fashion.

In the eight seconds or so for which the car is at rest, up to 21 perfectly drilled crew members work in perfect harmony to get the job completed. The driver keeps his right foot firmly on the brake and, within a second of the car stopping, the jacks go under the front and rear of the car. Simultaneously, one mechanic per wheel attaches the compressed air wheel gun to the central nut locating that wheel on its hub.

By the time a second mechanic has physically removed the wheel, 1.6s will have passed since the car has stopped. A third mechanic on each corner fits a replacement wheel and tyre only 2.2s into the stop; the wheels are fully tightened in 4.2s and the locking pins positioned in 5.2s.

While this work is proceeding, two more mechanics are in control of the refuelling line which attaches to a quick-release connection on the side of the fuel cell, with a third operating the refuelling rig itself. This task is completed 7.7s after the car first rolled to a halt and the refuelling hose is duly removed. The refuelling rigs are supplied by the FIA with the same controlled flow rate for all teams, which allows reasonably accurate calculations for consumption purposes.

From the front of the car, the chief mechanic keeps a watchful eye on the refuelling process, only signalling the driver back into the race when he is satisfied that all the various tasks have been completed with flawless precision.

The moment the refuelling hose is removed *(left)*, Villeneuve drops the clutch . . .

TIMING (seconds)

0.0	Car stops
0.3	Refuelling hose is attached
1.0	Car raised on its jacks
1.6	Old wheels removed
2.2	New wheels on
4.2	Wheels fully tightened
5.2	Locking pins positioned
7.7	Refuelling hose removed
8.0	GO!

. . . and is accelerating hard on his way as the pit crew breathes again.

The Feedback from Racing

Proof of the strength of the modern-day F1 car is offered by the way Alexander Wurz emerged unhurt from his barrel-roll in Montreal at the start of the 1998 Canadian Grand Prix.

Constructional safety has been the hallmark of Grand Prix cars since the early 1980s when McLaren designer John Barnard evolved the first carbon-fibre composite chassis design for the team that would go on to dominate the F1 winner's rostrum for much of the following decade.

Obviously a degree of luck plays a part in the outcome of any accident, whether on road or race track, but for the past decade or more, Grand Prix car design has been tailored to offer the occupants of these precision-built, high-speed projectiles the best possible chance of survival in the event of a catastrophic accident.

This has been done not only by ensuring the cars are manufactured from the most sophisticated space-age materials, such as carbon-fibre composite, but also by subjecting them to a rigorous programme of impact testing before they are permitted to race. This year safety levels have been further enhanced to provide additional lateral head protection for the drivers, a long-term development which has flowed from the death of three-times World Champion Ayrton Senna in the 1994 San Marino GP.

Senna's Williams survived a 150 mph impact against a concrete retaining wall with its carbon-fibre monocoque intact, but the Brazilian driver sustained a fatal blow from flying front suspension debris torn from his own car. This accident, followed by the serious head injuries to Austrian driver Karl Wendlinger in practice for the same year's Monaco GP, set designers thinking in terms of increased head protection.

'Performance and safety are probably the two most important concerns in your mind when you sit down to design a car,' says Gary Anderson, the Jordan F1 team's technical director. 'You want your driver to be as quick as possible, and as safe as possible.

'Motor racing does have inherent dangers, as was demonstrated when Martin Brundle crashed one of our cars spectacularly at Melbourne in 1996. The difference between Martin hurting himself in that accident, and not hurting himself, is partly down to luck. You never know where bits of the car are going to end up, or whether another driver is going to hit you in that situation.

The aftermath of Ayrton Senna's fatal crash at Imola in 1994. Although the monocoque of his Williams withstood a massive impact with a concrete wall in impressive fashion, the Brazilian sustained severe head injuries.

87

'You can, however, devise regulations to ensure that the drivers are safe in as many situations as possible, hence the new regulation concerning cockpits. As far as our cockpit sides are concerned, safety was the first thing we looked at because that, after all, is the reason that the latest regulations were introduced in the first place.'

Motor racing's governing body, the FIA, not only has responsibility for administering the sport, but also has a persuasive voice when it comes to debating road car safety standards in the European parliament. Although the performance of a Grand Prix car differs enormously from that of its road-going equivalent, FIA President Max Mosley believes that there are specific areas where motor racing can assist road car safety developments.

The most obvious example of this process is the FIA's wide-ranging support for tough new child safety-seat legislation based on the innovative ISOFIX system, which members of the European parliament are lobbying car manufacturers to provide mounting points for in all their new models.

'This is a classic example where work in Formula 1 is having a direct spin-off for road safety for ordinary people, in this case for children,' said Mosley. 'The idea of current F1 research is to take the driver and seat out together in the event of an accident so you don't aggravate any injuries. That led naturally to thoughts of child seats and our discussions on ISOFIX.'

The FIA's initiative has also resulted in new impact testing standards for road cars being introduced by the European parliament which, once fully implemented, could prevent 90,000 deaths and serious injuries in the EU each year. These standards were required for new cars from October 1998.

Although it is difficult to draw any direct parallels between motor racing crash tests and those applied to road cars, the FIA believes the stimulus of F1 engineering innovation can only have a positive effect on the way in which road car safety is tackled into the next millennium.

The cars are now fitted with padded cockpit sides to protect their drivers in the event of a heavy impact. Bulky padding of the kind seen on Michael Schumacher's Ferrari in 1996 *(opposite)* has given way to the less obvious protection afforded by Jarno Trulli's 1998 Prost *(below)*.

4
chapter

WHAT MAKES THE DRIVERS TICK?

Michael Schumacher is regarded as the best, particularly by team-mate Eddie Irvine *(right)*.

Grand Prix drivers are intensely committed, immensely determined sportsmen. Yet while they are all driven by much the same basic competitive instinct, putting a finger on what motivates their capacity to stretch themselves to the outer limit of sporting achievement is not always an easy task. Using a handful of examples, in this chapter we try to identify the recipe for Grand Prix success, before examining the huge contribution to driver safety made by the FIA Medical Delegate Professor Sid Watkins.

What Makes a Driver Special

Eddie Irvine is probably the person best qualified to pass comment on Michael Schumacher's talents. Since the start of the 1996 season he has filled the most unenviable, yet at the same time envied, position in the F1 business: driving the second Ferrari alongside the man who has now firmly grasped the late Ayrton Senna's crown as the greatest racing driver of his generation.

'I have never seen anyone in a racing car like him,' said Irvine. 'Even Senna couldn't do what Michael does. He is so quick straight out, on the first lap. I know I can never be World Champion in the same team as Michael.'

After the 1997 French Grand Prix at Magny-Cours, Schumacher confessed he could for the first time see a realistic chance of becoming Ferrari's first World Champion driver since 1979. With three wins in the previous four races, he seemed poised to press home his attack with the flair which the Italian team's technical director Ross Brawn believes is unique among contemporary F1 stars.

'The main thing you quickly realise about Michael is that he brings so much logic and brain power to bear on the business of driving a Grand Prix car,' said Brawn, who previously worked with him at Benetton during his 1994 and '95 championship-winning seasons.

'He will analyse what a car is doing and report back precisely what he believes could be improved, and any change to the set-up immediately results in him going faster. That is enormously satisfying for an engineer. He can also record every detail of how a car behaves through a corner, for example, and while the telemetry systems we have at our disposal these days are pretty impressive, it often comes down to talking to the driver to make real progress.

'For example, the telemetry may tell us that the car is understeering on the turn-in to a corner, translating into oversteer as the driver gets on the throttle on the exit. But what Michael can tell us is which of these characteristics is costing him the most time.

'He has also changed slightly in terms of his approach since he joined Ferrari,' Brawn continues, 'perhaps displaying a little more independence, which, I suspect, is a product of having to fend for himself in 1996, his first year with Ferrari, which is a team that tends to involve its drivers more closely in deciding how the car is developing than perhaps we did when we were at Benetton.

'There is no question in my mind that he is easily the best driver I have ever worked with, although I have to say I never had the opportunity to work with either Alain Prost or Ayrton Senna. But Michael is clearly in the same sort of class.'

Opposite: Schumacher, the all-round sportsman with the irrepressible competitive spirit. *Above:* Top dogs. Two of the most influential people in the F1 business: Ferrari sporting director Jean Todt and star driver Michael Schumacher.

The Pragmatic Approach

For his part, McLaren-Mercedes driver David Coulthard believes that there is less complexity about the business of Grand Prix racing than many might have it. It is extremely demanding and highly competitive, but the bottom line is hard work and commitment with the machinery you have been given.

'There is no rocket science involved here,' he says. 'It's a car, driver and team. If it all gels and you do your job, the results will be there.

'There is always pressure to perform. But I want to perform. When I was at Williams in 1995, a lot of people felt happy when I finished second, but I couldn't feel good about that sort of result because I knew I had not performed at my best.'

Coulthard reflects on 1995 as something of a missed opportunity. He had been promoted to the full-time race team in preference to Nigel Mansell and most observers had high hopes for him in his first full season driving the best car in the F1 business.

Yet it never quite gelled. The lingering effects of tonsillitis took the edge off his driving in the first part of the year and, by the time he had found his feet to score a commanding win in the Portuguese Grand Prix at Estoril, his place alongside Damon Hill in 1996 had been taken by Jacques Villeneuve. Of such misfortunes are crucial opportunities made – and sometimes squandered.

'Yet I only finished ten points behind Damon in the 1995 World Championship, despite my physical problems and an unforced error when I slid into the pit wall at Adelaide coming in for my first pit stop while leading the race,' he reflects.

'With that in mind, if I had still been in a Williams, I do believe I would have won the 1996 World Championship.'

Opposite: David Coulthard: cool, calm and logical.

Above: Coulthard had control of the opening race of the 1998 season in Australia but stuck to an agreement that allowed team-mate Mika Häkkinen the win after the Finn had led through the first corner.

The Feel-good Factor

Damon Hill is a driver who believes that the 'feel good' factor is a matter of enormous importance for the average Grand Prix driver – and that many F1 team owners simply do not understand what is needed to coax the best out of their high-priced investments behind the wheel of their racing cars.

'For example, I put an enormous amount of pressure on myself in 1995,' he says, 'but I think I've come to realise that there are some things that you just can't control, so you just have to do the best you can and prepare well. I think I was better prepared in 1996 and felt happier for it.'

Hill neatly sidestepped any debate on the question of the Williams team's lack of psychological support for its drivers when they are out of the cockpit, a shortcoming which has been freely acknowledged by Frank Williams himself.

'I think it is true to say that Benetton, for example, appear to understand very well that some drivers need that cosseting and feel-good factor to get the best out of themselves,' he says. 'Yet I think the feel-good factor comes as much from the driver as anything. I think I've now recognised that if I feel good, then the team feels good and we all benefit. When things aren't going so well, everyone is looking around for somebody who is going to get them out of the hole. I think I was better equipped to do that in 1996 than I was with all the trouble in '95. I felt more comfortable with the responsibility than before.'

Opposite: Damon Hill; a believer in the feel-good factor. He confirmed the value of unshakeable self-belief in 1996 *(below)* when he won the World Championship with Williams.

Commitment to the Team

Opposite: Mika Häkkinen; a long road to the top of the world.

Above: Mika produced a faultless drive to win in Monaco, just one of the highlights of the Finn's attack on the 1998 World Championship.

McLaren-Mercedes star Mika Häkkinen believes that the closer the relationship between a driver and the team he drives for, the better the performance of both parties will be.

Häkkinen, of course, is one of the very few F1 drivers who has made a full recovery from an extremely serious accident. Practising for the 1995 Australian GP, he crashed his McLaren MP4/10B heavily following a left-rear tyre deflation as he turned into the 110 mph, fourth-gear right-hander leading onto Adelaide's long Brabham Straight.

The car spun wildly over a high kerb into a single row of protective tyres facing the concrete barrier on the outside of the corner. Häkkinen's life was saved by doctors who performed an emergency tracheotomy at the trackside in order to prevent any brain damage through oxygen loss.

'Certainly I had some situations in 1996 when I was thinking that perhaps I shouldn't be so tired, I should be more fresh, and that this might have been a consequence of the accident,' he reflected in 1997. 'Yet the 100 per cent maximum commitment never left me. And I was supported flat-out by all the people around me. In such difficult conditions that support was mega-important. And I don't mean sympathy or pity. A kick in the bum sometimes, that's what you need.

'There have been several occasions where we have come close, but I don't reflect on things in that way. At the end of the day, the only reason I am here is to win the World Championship and that's what counts. So I am going to work flat-out to get to that point.

'The ambition is to get through winter testing really strong. Not just quickest in the occasional test, but setting the pace throughout. If you are one second off the pace, then you think, "Well, perhaps we're in a position to win maybe a race or two."

'But if you can absolutely set the pace, your mind clicks and you go like a bull. Now we have got to the point that the car is that good, so I am very, very confident.'

'It's not a question of how many races you win, whether you scored three points or four points at this or that race. The real question is what are the lap times? Are they quickest, or not? If you are not quickest, you have a hell of a lot of work. If you are quickest, you still have a hell of a lot of work.'

1998
FORMULA 1
WORLD
CHAMPIONSHIP
BRIDGESTONE
WARSTEINER
sparco

If the Worst Comes to the Worst

Grand Prix drivers go about their business today knowing that they are less likely to be involved in a fatal accident than at any time in the history of the sport.

Standards of car construction and circuit safety have been transformed beyond belief over the past two decades. In the 1960s, if a Formula 1 car crashed, the chances were that it would burst into flames, or, at the very least, its chassis of aluminium sheeting would crumple around the driver and cause serious injury.

One man can take a large slice of the credit for the improved medical facilities at race circuits across the globe. He is Professor Sid Watkins, one of the world's most eminent neuro-surgeons and a passionate motor racing fan. He was originally recruited 20 years ago for the role by Bernie Ecclestone and has attended virtually every round of the F1 World Championship ever since.

Watkins is universally known as 'The Prof' among his friends and colleagues. He was also one of Ayrton Senna's closest personal friends and recounts that, after Roland Ratzenberger had been killed during qualifying for the 1994 San Marino Grand Prix, he felt that he had to tell Senna precisely what he thought about the risks involved in the sport.

'Ayrton,' he said, 'why don't you withdraw from racing tomorrow? I don't think you should do it [the race]. In fact, why don't you give it up altogether. What else do you need to do? You have been World Champion three times, you are obviously the quickest driver. Give it up and let's go fishing.'

'He was silent,' Professor Watkins recalls. 'I went on: "I don't think the risk is worth continuing – pack it in." He gave me a very steady look and, now calm, he said: "Sid, there are certain things over which we have no control. I cannot quit. I have to go on."

'Those were the last words he ever said to me.'

There is no doubt that Watkins feels that Senna was one of the most remarkable drivers he has ever met. His death, while leading the San Marino race in his Williams barely 24 hours after this conversation, had a profound effect on this otherwise detached and very pragmatic medical man.

Sid Watkins has had a long-time interest in motor racing ever since he completed his Army service in 1956. He had done some medical assistance work in his spare time at various British club racing circuits and was a close friend of Dean Delamont, then the very popular chief of the RAC Motor Sports Division. But it was while The Prof was in America, working as a neuro-surgeon at Syracuse, New York State, from 1962 through to 1970 that he really began to take a serious interest in motor racing medicine, attending events at Watkins Glen, home of the United States GP.

'My approach was to take a team of people who would be sufficiently clinically senior and experienced to make a pretty good diagnosis of any injuries on the spot and, if something had to be done, be in a position to do it,' he explained.

'Anyway, in 1970 I came back to London at 42 years old and Dean Delamont asked me to get involved as a member of the RAC Medical Panel.'

Thereafter, he gradually expanded his experience until May 1978 when Bernie Ecclestone came to see him. 'This contact was again through Dean Delamont,' he explained, 'and Bernie asked me whether I would think about coming to all the F1 races and try to set certain minimum medical standards at the tracks. So I said OK, and the next week I went to meet the drivers and decided that I would give it a go.'

Prof Watkins found that the medical standards were, by and large, pretty low at most circuits at that time. One of the worst examples he found was at Brands Hatch.

'If you came off the circuit anywhere you had to get back to the pits or the paddock and then go under a tunnel, up an access road behind the stands,' he remembers with a frown.

Above: The cream of the world's driving talent, safe in the knowledge that every conceivable measure has been taken to ensure their safety.

Opposite: The Montreal pit lane is unusually quiet, but the safety and medical cars are there, ready for when the action starts.

'Then you found the medical centre was a small set of rooms underneath the main grandstand at the back. It was very difficult to gain access to with anybody who was sick. When I went in, I asked the two ambulancemen – who were sharing a pint of beer – what they would do in the event of needing oxygen from the oxygen cylinder, and they looked around the place to try and find the key to open it. When they found it, and opened it, they found there wasn't anything in it. So those were the standards.

'Medical centres were generally quite primitive, or didn't even exist. When we went to Imola for the first time we worked in tents. Today, that circuit has a wonderful medical centre.'

A Crucial Medical Network

Ecclestone was sufficiently shrewd to realise that Watkins's connections within the medical profession would be enormously beneficial in setting up a global F1 system of medical assistance.

The Prof smiles. 'The neuro-surgical population of the world is not enormous,' he explains. 'Take Britain, for example. We used to have just one neuro-surgeon per million of the population – now perhaps it is two per million.

Opposite: **The Mercedes-Benz medical car: always ready to attend the scene of an accident.**
Below: **The medical centre at Silverstone is equipped for almost any emergency.**

'What this means is that there is a sort of neuro-surgical "mafia" – people who trained with me in England or the USA are now in Argentina or South Africa or Australia. And with colleagues and friends like this I was able to put something together on the Old Boy network, if you like, before the formal FIA Medical Commission was established.'

As far as the Imola tragedy is concerned, Professor Watkins clearly finds it difficult to talk about what happened in detail. After the Ratzenberger accident in Saturday qualifying he was very concerned not only about Senna's temperamental state, but also the general mood of the weekend. As a practical and analytical man, Watkins clearly does not believe in bad luck as a tangible element in itself, but he did express the view to the pace car driver after the opening lap of the race that he was apprehensive and would not be surprised if there was another accident.

When signalled out onto the circuit after the Senna crash, he knew full well who was involved the moment he saw the Williams at the trackside as he accelerated through Tamburello. He keeps his emotions private as he explains that he quickly appreciated the extent of Ayrton's injuries.

'I lifted his helmet visor and could see immediately that he had a very serious injury to his head,' he says quietly. 'He was deeply unconscious and it was obvious that he would have to be removed to hospital in as short a time as possible. But we lifted him onto the side of the circuit and he gave a short sigh. That was the point that, I believe, he left us for ever.'

Although no brain activity could be detected, Ayrton's heart continued to beat until just after 18.00 in the evening when he was officially declared dead at the Bologna hospital to which he had been evacuated by helicopter almost four hours earlier.

The Prof admits this was one of the most difficult days of his life, but, despite this, his love for motor racing continues unabated. He is now 69 years old, but displays an almost boyish and sustained enthusiasm for the sport which has been such a central part of his life for so long.

After spending many years as the head of the London Hospital's neuro-surgery department, Professor Watkins retired from the British National Health Service a couple of years ago and now practises privately in semi-retirement. This has obviously enabled him to concentrate more time on F1 as President of the FIA Expert Advisory Group which is investigating enhanced safety systems such as cockpit airbags for the future.

Prof Watkins regards safety and medical facilities as the area in which the most dramatic progress has been made within motor racing during the time that he has been involved with the sport.

'If you go and look at the medical centre at most circuits now,' he says, 'they've got everything you need to deal with a life-threatening situation. Some have basic operating theatres with all the advanced technology available. The facilities at many of these circuits are now superior to some hospitals you find in the outside world!'

chapter 5 THE TEAM OWNERS

Heavy traffic; the first corner of the '98 Spanish Grand Prix. The opening moments of the race are a time of great tension for the team owners, who have invested huge sums of money to put two cars on the starting grid.

In this chapter we take a look at a cross-section of F1 team owners and their own personal motivations. The competitiveness and determination radiated by these men is scarcely less intense than that displayed by the drivers they employ. Indeed, most have started out their motor racing careers as drivers, only for choice, circumstance, good fortune or a combination of all three to have taken them along this particular route.

In many ways, today's breed of F1 team owner deserves more respect than the men who put their lives on the line in the thick of the Grand Prix action. Certainly, the commercial, financial and technological complexities of operating such an organisation require more wide-ranging talents than those deployed by the drivers, most of whom have necessarily developed qualities of self-reliance – and indeed considerable selfishness – as they scramble towards the pinnacle of their personal achievement.

The Passionate Enthusiast

Veteran team chief Ken Tyrrell
(left) doesn't like what he's
hearing from Bernie Ecclestone.
Opposite: The clouds of smoke
signal an engine failure for
Takagi's Tyrrell and another bill in
a sport where money is consumed
at staggering rates in the quest
for victory.

When people use the word 'passion' in connection with motor racing they frequently use the term too loosely. Commitment, professionalism and attention to detail are some of the words which we regularly apply to these men, but 'passion' is not one to throw around too often. Yet that is exactly the word to describe Ken Tyrrell's life as a Grand Prix team owner. His passionate enthusiasm for Grand Prix racing remained undimmed long after the team's glory days were but a distant glimmer in the history books. When the Tyrrell family finally severed its connection with the team only months after selling out for a reputed £18 million to British American Racing at the end of 1997, Ken seemed like a man who had lost all his purpose in life. At 73 years of age, he was still passionate about the sport that had become his obsession.

'Originally I didn't follow motor racing, but in 1951 the local football team at Ockham in Surrey, for which I used to play, got a coach trip together to go to Silverstone,' he recalls, 'but it could just as easily have been a trip to the seaside at Brighton or Bognor.

'But we went to Silverstone, the meeting when the BRM raced for the first time, and I remember a horrific queue going through Buckingham – it was several miles south of the town –

but we eventually arrived. I sat in the grandstand at Stowe and watched my first motor race meeting.

'The supporting race was for 500 cc F3 cars and one of the competitors was a guy called Alan Brown who I saw from the programme came from Guildford, where I lived at that time. So when I got home, I went round and knocked on Alan Brown's door and said, "I saw you racing at Silverstone, sir – could I see your car?"

'Well, he kept his car in a large garage in the garden of a nursery which his mother ran. So he showed me round the car, told me a little bit about it, and at the end of the year I bought it from him. And became a racing driver!'

Ken went off to test the car for the first time at the old anti-clockwise Brands Hatch circuit – before the Druids loop had been built. 'Alan Brown told me if I couldn't get round in 60 seconds, or whatever it was, then I should sell the car,' says Ken. 'Well, I had several spins, but eventually got inside that time at the end of the day. So I was hooked.'

Ken raced through much of the 1950s, eventually going into partnership with Alan Brown and Cecil Libowitz in 1958 to run a pair of Cooper F2 cars on an international basis. 'When eventually I discovered I could only finish fifth, sixth or seventh at this level, it didn't satisfy me,' he recalls.

'Then on one occasion I loaned the car to Michael Taylor at Aintree and he drove much better than I did. So I decided that team management was my particular slot.'

Ken has always been self-effacing when it comes to his reputation as a talent spotter, yet in fact he is doing himself rather less than justice. 'It's not really true, you see,' he grins broadly. 'It sounds all right when you read it in print, but it's not really like that.

'If you go back to 1960, when I started running my own Formula Junior team with loaned Cooper chassis and BMC engines, I had John Surtees and Henry Taylor and we won races all over Europe. Most of the people we were racing against were owner/drivers competing for fun, but I was free to sign up whoever I thought was the best driver.

'John Surtees, Henry Taylor, John Love, Timmy Mayer – they were all very good. Then came Jackie [Stewart], of course, and his talent was so blindingly obvious it didn't take a talent spotter to discern it.'

Jackie Stewart's relationship with Tyrrell was magic. Ken recalls they fell out only once. 'It was at an Oulton Park Gold Cup when Jackie was complaining bitterly about whatever car we had there,' he recalls, 'and I do remember we had a few words. But we never fell out over money!

'He drove for me in F3, F2 and then F1, but the only time we had a written contract was in the first year.'

Jackie won three World Championships for Ken, the first in the Tyrrell-entered Matra in 1969, the second and third with Ken's own cars in 1971 and '73. He had hoped to sustain the momentum of that great partnership into 1974, promoting Jackie's team-mate François Cevert to the team leadership after Stewart's retirement. Sadly, Cevert was killed practising for the 1973 US Grand Prix at Watkins Glen and the link was broken.

'François absolutely worshipped Jackie as his idol,' recalls Ken. 'I remember Jackie's last F1 win, in the '73 German GP at the Nürburgring, where they finished in 1-2 formation. At the end of the race he stepped out of the car and said, "François could have passed me any time he liked. He was flat quicker than I was."

'But the point was that François stayed in his wheel tracks because he still felt he had a lot to learn from Jackie. And, of course, he knew that Jackie was retiring at the end of the year, and that his time would come.'

Despite his age, Ken Tyrrell could never be described as a nostalgic old fogey. 'Apart from this slight problem we're currently having over the Concorde Agreement, I love F1 as passionately as ever,' he said with feeling in 1997. 'It has got better all the time to the point where it is now an extremely successful global sport.

'I suppose you could say that I regret the fact that F1 has changed inasmuch as, when I started, you could simply go up to Cosworth at Northampton, buy a Cosworth DFV and, assuming you had a good car and a decent driver, it had the chance of winning the next Grand Prix. And not just the next Grand Prix, but races for the next six or seven years.

'I regret the demise of that part of F1, because nowadays engines are so critical, and the disparity between them is so great, that it's not quite how we would want it to be.

'But, apart from this, I really have no nostalgia for the so-called good old days!'

Tyrrell is outwardly an unobtrusive and pragmatic man. Before his family took the decision to sell up, the team was run for many years on minimal sponsorship. This involved a financial balancing act which many others have sought to imitate and failed dramatically in their efforts. Tyrrell survived because he never spent a penny more than he had in the bank.

The Tyrrell name is expected to disappear at the end of the 1998 season as part of Craig Pollock's ambitious plans to set up a new team under the British American Racing banner.

The Committed Perfectionist

Ron Dennis, McLaren's driving force and a man who believes he knows the formula for F1 success better than most.

McLaren International founder Ron Dennis had a pretty clear idea of how he wanted his business to develop from the moment he left his job as chief mechanic on the Brabham F1 team at the end of 1970 to start up on his own.

In 1971 Dennis and colleague Neil Trundle set up their own Formula 2 team and this provided a crucial springboard for Dennis's long-term ambitions. High standards of preparation and turn-out were absolutely central to the Rondel Racing credo and set the tone for everything which was to follow throughout Dennis's business career in motor racing.

He frankly admits that he even put the idea of getting married consciously on hold until he was firmly established as a successful businessman and team owner, even if the fact that he now has a young family in his early fifties makes him a little nervous and uneasy.

Dennis took control of the ailing McLaren F1 team in 1980 and revived its fortunes to brilliant effect, World Championship titles following in 1984, '85, '86, '88, '89, '90 and '91. This was followed by a dramatic performance slump from which the team successfully emerged in 1997, in partnership with engine supplier Mercedes-Benz, and another World Championship seems firmly on the cards in 1998.

'I have a belief that everything is important in life and everything is important when you are trying to achieve high levels of success in any business – certainly in Formula 1,' says Dennis.

'I believe that at all times you should have the best – or at least try to have the best. This is not simply about money, it is mainly about commitment. We try to instil it into the very fibre of everyone's approach to their work for the team.'

It is this basic inspiration which underpins every aspect of his whole operation. Not only the racing team, but also the new technology centre which he plans to build close to the current factory near Woking, where he intends to continue building high-quality cars for many years to come.

'Winning is not just about winning on the circuit, it is also about winning off the circuit,' he explains. 'Consequently, when people pass less-than-favourable remarks about the things that we do, most of the time those remarks broadly reflect the fact that they recognise that we have higher standards than they have achieved.

'Motor sport is not about the short term, it is about the long term. While we were taking the blows that had been administered to us by our fellow competitors and the media during our thin years between 1993 and '96, I have said, "Well, they don't understand." We have been in a position of dominance in the past and we will regain that position in the future.

'The problem is that many observers fail to understand the complexity of Formula 1 motor racing. The top twenty tennis players at Wimbledon could borrow each other's rackets and probably play within a very small percentage of how they played with their own.'

Dennis is particularly adept at lateral thinking and projects a shrewd understanding of Grand Prix racing which extends beyond the simple, obvious scenario of cars running round a circuit. Unlike many of his contemporaries in the ranks of F1 team owners, he also understands that success in F1 may involve playing what he habitually describes as 'the long game'.

In essence that means any improvements and enhancements McLaren might make to its design and manufacturing infrastructure. In brief, there is no short-cut to success. It involves sustained hard work and self-belief which can be made more frustrating by the inherent complexity of the Grand Prix machine.

'When you look at many sports, you realise that the role the equipment plays in the overall equation is very small,' he explains. 'By contrast, a Grand Prix car is one of the most complex pieces of

Secrecy is the watchword; McLaren ensures that the details of the MP4/13's rear wing are not subject to photographic scrutiny.

equipment you could ever place in the hands of a sportsman. That is what sets motor racing apart, and why it is so enormously difficult to win a Grand Prix.

'We have very much a desire to win as many races as possible. The simple fact is that you win Grands Prix and World Championships not by considering the next race, or even the race after that, but you do it by means of what you plan for the future.

'Our approach with Mercedes is many years into the future, to try and give our respective engineering groups the very best facilities for them to contribute to us winning races. To make it possible, you have to have everybody around you with the same long-term vision. We are trying to develop a long-term strategy to win consistently, both for McLaren and Mercedes, both of whom have a distinguished heritage.'

THE TEAM OWNERS

The man behind the Mercedes V10. Ilmor boss Mario Illien heads the company which built the best Grand Prix engine of the 1998 season – a huge investment for the German car maker, but one which guarantees sufficient exposure to represent hard commercial sense.

Long Slog from Obscurity

Contrast Ken Tyrrell's business credo with the financially *avant garde* management techniques practised by Frank Williams in the mid-1970s. Williams was another frustrated racer who scrimped and saved his way into the F3 milieu in the 1960s, eventually retiring because he realised he would not make the Big Time. He had, he reasoned, more of a future as a team owner.

Yet Williams, who today heads up one of the most consistently successful F1 teams of all time, makes no secret of the fact that he had no grand plan. He just lived on his wits, making his arrangements by thinking on his feet and working out how to tackle the next challenge when he was confronted by it, no earlier.

This spontaneous approach led him into Formula 1 at the start of the 1969 season fielding a private Brabham-Ford for his close friend Piers Courage, a member of the famous brewing family. Even though Courage took the Williams team's Brabham to second places in both the Monaco and United States Grands Prix that season, Williams freely confessed he still felt a touch overawed by the whole motor racing business.

In the summer of the following year Frank's world was brutally shattered when Courage was killed at the wheel of his team's de Tomaso in the Dutch Grand Prix. The disaster served as a cruel reminder that motor racing has its hard and uncompromising edge.

Yet Williams kept the raw surface of his emotion under firm control and fought back. Despite everincreasing financial problems over the next few years, he held his nerve. Eventually he sold his company and started off again at the bottom of the F1 ladder in 1977 with a private off-the-peg March.

Opposite: Frank Williams, team owner and F1 enthusiast *par excellence.*

The new enterprise made its debut at Silverstone for the British Grand Prix; two years later, Frank's team would be celebrating its first F1 victory at the very same race.

It was the start of an era which would see one Grand Prix victory after another cascade into the record books. Yet Williams never took success for granted. Watching his cars winning races seemed to have a narcotic effect on the team boss. The more victories the team achieved, the more he wanted.

This utter single-minded focus and resolve helped Frank on two further occasions when his life was touched by tragedy. In the spring of 1986 a road accident in the south of France saw him sustain spinal injuries which have confined him to a wheelchair ever since. Eight years later, Ayrton Senna, a man he deified and who was just starting out on his Williams F1 career, was fatally injured in the San Marino Grand Prix at Imola.

There is a no-nonsense ethos at Williams Grand Prix Engineering which accurately reflects the personalities of the company founder and his partner, the company's technical director Patrick Head. This is an attitude which suffuses the senior management of most Grand Prix teams, although the ability not to waver from a chosen course when under the most intense pressure imaginable is absolutely vital.

Eddie Jordan: One of a New Breed

F1 is all about media coverage; if you can't win, there are other ways of achieving it. Jordan found that Emma Noble's presence in the pit lane guaranteed their sponsors plenty of exposure.

For his part, Eddie Jordan may be a generation younger than Tyrrell, but his motivation was much the same. A competent and competitive racer, he made his mark in F3, but was slightly handicapped by the fact that he was older than his contemporary rivals.

Even though it seemed as though Eddie was on the threshold of a successful professional racing career, he took the bold decision to retire from the cockpit to concentrate on operating his own Formula 3 team, a challenge which inevitably led to managing the careers of many of the young drivers who raced for him.

In 1983, Martin Brundle drove an Eddie Jordan Racing Ralt to second place in the British F3 Championship, locked in battle for much of the year with Brazilian rising star Ayrton Senna. Four years later Johnny Herbert won that same title for Jordan. In between, 'EJ' honed his business reputation as a shrewd operator, laying the foundations of what would eventually become the most promising new F1 team to arrive on the scene for several years.

When the new Formula 3000 category was introduced for 1985, Jordan quickly focused on it not only as a racing category in itself, but also as a training ground for drivers signed up by his own management company. Eddie's true forte as a business manager was perhaps best demonstrated in 1989 when he recruited the young Frenchman Jean Alesi to race alongside Martin Donnelly in his F3000 squad. When Tyrrell F1 driver Michele Alboreto left the team in mid-season after a row over clashing cigarette sponsors, he successfully placed Alesi in the vacant cockpit on a three-year deal. Alesi quickly established himself as something of a star in 1990 and then had his head turned by lucrative offers from Ferrari for the following season. That meant Ferrari negotiating a release from his contract with Tyrrell, but Jordan's company still took its percentage of Alesi's reputed $6 million fee from the Italian team, around $600,000.

Jordan certainly needed the money. For 1991 he decided to take the plunge into F1. He knew the sport inside out and committed his operation to a lease deal with Cosworth Engineering which would enable his new team to use supplies of the trusty Ford HB V8 engine during its fledgling season.

Yet Jordan was prepared to go to the very brink in order to survive. This quality of ferocious determination among team owners arises time and time again. They are prepared to put their homes, all their worldly possessions, firmly on the line in an attempt to make the Big Time.

'In my particular case – which I suppose is true to many Irish people – I was brought up mentally geared to securing a safe job,' he admits. 'I started out as the epitome of that philosophy: job for life in banking, do the Institute of Bankers exams, boost it up with an accountancy degree. All the way through the state school system, play golf . . .

'But my attraction to motor racing changed all that. It became as addictive as a drug. I could see that the way my parents had brought me up represented the preparation for a well-structured, conventional life. My father was an accountant and I was their only son.'

Jordan is so immersed in today and tomorrow that he hasn't much time for history, variously explaining that his enthusiasm for motor racing was fired 'possibly by watching the Monaco Grand Prix on television' but also by the rallying activities of his uncle, Noel Smith, who drove a Mini Cooper S to great effect in Irish national events during the mid-1960s. Yet it was a banking strike in Ireland, believe it or not, in late 1967 which provided the crucial opportunity, triggering a sequence of events which brought him into motor racing full-time. He worked for the Jersey Electricity Company during the day and in a bar six evenings a week. But on his days off he spent all his time at the Ste Brelades karting track. The bug bit!

Fast forward 30 years and close scrutiny of the Jordan team's CV may make promising reading,

Close shave; Damon Hill's Jordan-Mugen Honda strays from the straight and narrow.

but its proprietor is well aware that it is performance which counts. Even after the start of the 1998 season, when the lack of performance from the team's Mugen Honda-engined cars driven by Damon Hill and Ralf Schumacher pitched it into a crisis situation, the feisty Dubliner believes that his team has the necessary qualities to survive and flourish where others have faltered and failed.

On the other hand, he makes no secret of his relief that Jordan Grand Prix has survived into the era where the financial pickings of expanded television revenue provide a handy financial bedrock on which to base his team's operations. At the 1998 Monaco Grand Prix, Jordan was one of ten teams to sign the new Concorde Agreement, which will govern the manner in which the sport is organised for the next ten years. As explained elsewhere, in return for an undertaking to compete in F1 during that period, the signatory teams are rewarded with television income ranging from $9.8 million to $23 million annually for the duration of the agreement.

'It's almost impossible for an F1 team to go bust now, and Eddie knows that as well as the next man,' commented a leading team manager. 'Effectively, this means that he's made it – even if he never wins a single race.'

Knowing which side one's bread is buttered in the minefield of F1 politics is another key factor for a team owner to keep in mind. Jordan is also politically very adept in this respect. Unlike McLaren,

Williams and Tyrrell, who spent almost two years refusing to sign the new Concorde Agreement, Jordan quickly signed up for what was being offered.

'The situation was very clear as far as I was concerned,' he says, 'although I am not saying that one was right and one was wrong. In 1991, I felt that Jordan had done a reasonable job and deserved a place in F1. The team was different; we had a different attitude, the whole thing had a bit of a buzz to it and the potential was always there.

'At that time F1 teams were beginning to fall out of the sky [in terms of going out of business]. Fondmetal, Brabham and Lotus were only a handful of those who did not survive much longer. It wasn't clear that we were then going to survive. Today the team structure is now so strong that I think it is very different.

'So why did I join those who signed the 1997 Concorde Agreement? I analysed it in detail. I had an old teacher once who told me that, when you are forced to make a decision very quickly, you need to fully understand the question you are considering. In this case, we had to ask two basic questions: (a) does it make the car go any better? and (b) if not, can it produce benefits in other ways?'

Even so, Jordan projects the image of a Bernie man. Yet he denies that he is beholden in any way to the FIA Vice-President, who, he admits, loaned him a seven-figure sum to balance the books after his financially precarious freshman F1 season.

Eddie rebuts this contention with some vehemence, moving forward in his seat and wagging his finger. Ecclestone's financial assistance towards struggling F1 teams has not, he claims, been limited to himself.

'Yes, Bernie has baled me out once,' he says with a stern directness. 'But I don't think there is a team in F1 that he hasn't either helped or baled out. That doesn't buy loyalty, but it helps in the decision-making process.'

Over the years, Eddie Jordan has displayed the Midas touch and proved extremely resilient. Faced with disappointment, he has developed the technique of putting on a light-hearted face and turning a humorous countenance to the watching world. Inevitably, this has laid him open to accusations that he is simply not serious enough about the task of achieving F1 success.

Those close to Jordan say that he is stung by such allegations, that the jocularity is a defence mechanism to cover a sense of bitter disappointment when his team fails to perform. Perhaps so, but the clock is now certainly ticking on the Jordan team's credibility. It can no longer afford to be 'best of the rest' or cast in a supporting role. It must deliver. No excuses. But those who suggest that Eddie Jordan is unaware of this situation probably misjudge him. Jordan, more than anybody else in his organisation, knows what has to be done.

'I am comfortable with the challenge' he says, 'and I'm rewarded on the basis of that, which has taken a huge part of the risk element out of my business. I've been in the risk business for nearly 30 years – heavy risk, risk which could have bankrupted me.

'By the end of 1991, I had spent 10 million [pounds]. I had just over three million coming in from buying and selling drivers, bits and pieces that I could put together, and three million from our group of sponsors.'

At this point, Jordan's lessons from the banking world paid off. 'If I had not had a fair degree of banking experience in terms of structuring a repayment campaign, it would have been so easy for me to have closed the book.

'Now we are out of that situation, but we still have to translate our efforts into hard results. We are sadly lacking so far, but even though we are only a short distance into the season, I am depressed that we have failed to amass more points to display where we really are.'

Playing for High Stakes

The survival of the Jordan team is a testament to Eddie's resilience. To outsiders, Jordan's next move made little sense. Simply in order to stay in business and keep racing, in 1992 he signed a contract for his team to use Japanese V12 Yamaha engines. From the touchlines, with no real knowledge of what was actually going on inside the Jordan empire, this looked like comfortable expediency.

'Eddie's only in it for the money,' chorused his critics. 'He's opted for a useless engine because he doesn't have to pay for it. And this after that promising start last year with the Ford V8s.' What wasn't clear at the time, of course, was that outstanding debts to Cosworth were part of that £4 million shortfall. Eddie drove himself to the verge of physical collapse as he toiled to sort out the mess.

By his own admission, he overdosed on caffeine and junk food. His cholesterol levels increased dramatically and, with characteristic immodesty, he admitted that he developed 'the most horrific piles you could imagine'. Yet he never, ever thought of throwing in the towel.

'For 22 years I had absolutely nothing and lived on a shoestring,' he confessed. 'Formula 1 gave me a big chance to make something realistic of my life and I wasn't going to blow it.'

Those early years of F1 survival were crucially buttressed by income from bringing on young drivers and selling on their contracts if the opportunity arose. Jordan's commercial director Ian Phillips explained the technique: 'When a new driver arrives in Formula 1, he usually pays for his seat in the car by bringing on board a sponsor. He will normally sign a two-year deal with the team plus an option for a third year. However, at the end of each season, the driver has a one-month period in which he can buy himself out of the contract for a sum agreed at the outset.

'In our early years, the buy-out was priced at somewhere between $4 and $5 million. Now it is around double that figure.' It therefore follows that when Eddie Irvine was bought out of his Jordan contract at the end of the 1995 season by Ferrari – a year ahead of its expiry – Jordan made a tidy profit from the deal.

Eddie Jordan is a naturally convivial character who hides an astute business edge beneath a veneer of amiability. He is also a survivor who is enjoying the trappings of wealth.

A Wider Canvas

For Tom Walkinshaw, chief of the Arrows F1 team, the original motivation for becoming immersed in the world of motor racing was much the same as Eddie Jordan's. Yet although the tough and gritty Scot had set out with the ambition of becoming a Grand Prix star, a combination of opportunity and circumstance would see him establishing one of the most formidable business empires within the international motor racing community.

After his initial single-seater hopes waned, Walkinshaw built himself a reputation as a respected saloon car racer, but more importantly also developed his talents for test and development work. His reputation in this area grew to the point where many private owners became willing to pay the Scot a daily fee to sort out their own saloon racers.

Tom was also extremely ambitious, with an eye for business opportunities, and it did not take long for him to realise there was a potential market to be tapped for those technical abilities. The first commercial signs of what would be a major shift of emphasis for the Scot came in 1976 when Tom Walkinshaw Racing was established on an industrial estate in the Oxford suburb of Kidlington.

In 1982 TWR commenced a long-standing partnership with Jaguar which saw their 5.3-litre XJS coupé developed to the point where Walkinshaw himself won the prestigious European Touring Car Championship two years later. Suitably encouraged, in 1985 Jaguar gave the green light for

Walkinshaw to develop a Le Mans winner. What followed was an intensive three-year programme of high technology development which saw TWR steadily raise the tempo of international sports car racing with a succession of superbly engineered XJR coupés.

In 1986 they won a single race, the Silverstone 1000 Km, and in 1987 TWR won the championship with eight wins out of ten races before adding Le Mans to their tally of victories in 1988. In the process, Jaguar's rather staid commercial image received a massive promotional boost which was reflected by an upsurge in showroom sales.

Walkinshaw's business dealings have not always ended happily. An ill-starred plan to establish a string of car dealerships – the Silverstone Motor Group – with the British Racing Drivers' Club, who own the British Grand Prix circuit, collapsed amidst legal acrimony in 1992. The breach between this bastion of motor racing tradition and the thrusting Scottish entrepreneur is, to this day, only slowly healing.

On the other hand, it was Walkinshaw's engineering expertise which enabled the Benetton team to raise the standard of its game, laying the solid foundations from which Michael Schumacher was able to win the 1994 and '95 World Championships. As part of this deal, forged in 1991, Walkinshaw's company took a shareholding in Benetton and the Scot took over the title of engineering director of

Eddie Jordan *(left)* and Tom Walkinshaw; both still seeking the F1 Big Time.

Walkinshaw's hopes of success are pinned on Mika Salo. The Finnish driver joined Arrows in 1998, having served a three-year apprenticeship with Tyrrell.

the F1 team. He was also a driving force in securing Schumacher's services for Benetton after the German driver's debut at the wheel of a Jordan in that year's Belgian Grand Prix. Some very persistent negotiations resulted in Michael making the move to Benetton – although Jordan threatened legal action at the time – and the rest, as they say, is history.

Yet although motor racing may be what TWR has become best known for thanks to its dramatic success in saloon and sports car racing across the world, the fact remains that the sport makes up only around ten per cent of the revenue generated by the group. The other 90 per cent comes from the road car work carried out by more than 1300 employees spread across the world in England, France, Sweden, Australia and the United States. The design and development of Jaguar's XJ220 supercar, the Aston Martin DB7 and the specialist Volvo C70 coupé have all been handled by the dynamic Scot's business empire. Tom swapped his driving overalls for a business suit at the end of 1984 and rules his domain with an iron fist in an iron glove. Famous racing drivers and journalists alike have been known to tremble under his dour and intimidating gaze.

Through his partnership with Benetton, Walkinshaw was also offered the opportunity to purchase the rival Ligier team, which had been bought in 1994 by Benetton team chief Flavio Briatore.

However, the plans fell through and Walkinshaw acquired a controlling interest in Arrows instead. Walkinshaw admits to a calculated and pragmatic business approach, regarding his £6 million purchase of the Arrows team as a technical showcase for the TWR automotive empire. The 51-year-old Scot aims to build Arrows into a winning force by the end of the decade. He is intolerant of failure and deeply committed to success, even though it will take around £20 million of commercial sponsorship annually to underpin his ambitions.

'We are not doing this for fun, we are doing it to create a team which will be capable of winning Grands Prix,' he explained, 'and I think we should have that by next year. That is one of the advantages of going the Arrows route, enabling us this year to prepare the team to be in a position to win, or at least be in the top three.

'TWR's main business is obviously in the motor industry and engineering in the automotive sector. That has to be our first priority, but our technology is displayed by our racing teams and F1 is of primary importance to us as a marketing tool. We don't see it as a profit centre. It is a performance centre for the entire TWR group.'

Wealthy Brazilian Pedro Diniz brings the team much-needed finance and, contrary to the impression given by this unfortunate excursion into a gravel trap, has developed into a more than competent performer.

chapter 6 THE COSTS AND REWARDS

In F1, money makes the wheels go around. How much does it cost to fund a modern-day F1 team? How is the money spent? What is the engine supplier's investment? And how much do the drivers get paid – if, indeed, they get paid at all?

Bernie Ecclestone's efforts in expanding the sport's television coverage have been absolutely central to the explosion of interest in F1 racing, which now yields simply massive income for drivers, for team owners and, in particular, for Ecclestone in his role as F1 Commercial Rights Holder.

Over the 16-race series, taking into account race broadcasts, additional programmes and news coverage, the World Championship attracts almost 300 million viewers per race across 160 countries. Good value, even for a title sponsor paying top dollar to a front-line team.

Yet the budgets required by the leading teams to maintain their competitiveness are simply huge. Over the past 20 years Grand Prix racing has probably benefited more than any other single sport from the enormous revenues available from cigarette sponsorship – in 1998 the Philip Morris Marlboro brand is believed to have picked up the tab for around £50 million of the Ferrari team's £85 million F1 budget – but increasing anti-tobacco legislation throughout the world has put such financing in jeopardy.

From Ferrari, the budgets are obviously smaller the further down the grid one travels. At the opposite end of the scale, Minardi's 'survival' budget is around £10 million, which means that, under the terms of the 1998 Concorde Agreement, it will derive about two-thirds of its overall financing (£6 million) from television income. Ferrari, with about £16 million annually from television, gains a lesser proportion of its finance from this source.

For those fortunate teams who have engine supply contracts, this effectively saves around £10–12 million annually. In 1997 Williams won its ninth constructors' championship using Renault V10s supplied free of charge on a works-supported basis. This season the team is using the same engines, but being charged £13 million in lease fees. It is a temporary arrangement designed to fill the gap until the new BMW F1 engine – together with an investment of about £20 million by the German company – becomes available to the British team on an exclusive basis in 2000.

High-tech business. Millions of pounds are spent each year in order to put two cars onto the Grand Prix grid.

Yet £13 million cannot buy the best F1 engine performance, as has been emphasised by the Williams team's disappointing form in 1998. Mercedes-Benz is believed to have invested around £30 million annually for the past three seasons raising the standards of its engine performance to achieve its current position as the prime World Championship contender.

The figures for developing a car, aside from its engine costs, are similarly daunting. Williams probably spends around £9 million researching, designing and building the six or so F1 chassis it uses during the course of the season. It will need somewhere in the region of £8 million for future research and development, around £15 million for the team's running costs at races and tests, £6 million for salaries and £10 million for driver retainers and associated costs plus £13 million for its Mecachrome lease fees. That is a total outgoing in the order of £61 million.

On the income side of the balance sheet the team probably earns £25 million from its title sponsor Winfield, plus a wide cross-section of associated backers which include Veltins (a German beer company), Sonax car care products, Henderson Investors, Andersen Consulting, Falke textiles and the German digital television channel. Williams Grand Prix Engineering made an operating profit of £6.6 million in 1995, the most recent year for which figures are available.

Most leading teams are similarly profitable but there is no clear indication whether the wealth and stratospheric income of Grand Prix motor racing as a whole will eventually lead to a stock exchange flotation of Bernie Ecclestone's F1 Holdings empire. Ecclestone has traditionally been a secretive businessman and may eventually decide that he is not prepared to have his business acumen laid open to the sort of scrutiny which goes hand-in-hand with a share flotation.

Keeping the customer satisfied. The Williams cars of Heinz-Harald Frentzen *(above)* and Jacques Villeneuve wore a bright new livery in 1998 following a change of sponsor.

Opposite, top: A lifetime of F1; Jackie Stewart *(right)* shares his thoughts with son Paul about the fortunes of their new Grand Prix team. The Stewart-Ford organisation's investment in F1 could be approaching £35 million during only its second season, placing a weighty burden on the shoulders of number one driver Rubens Barrichello *(opposite, bottom)*.

The adulation of the crowds is the driving force behind the business.

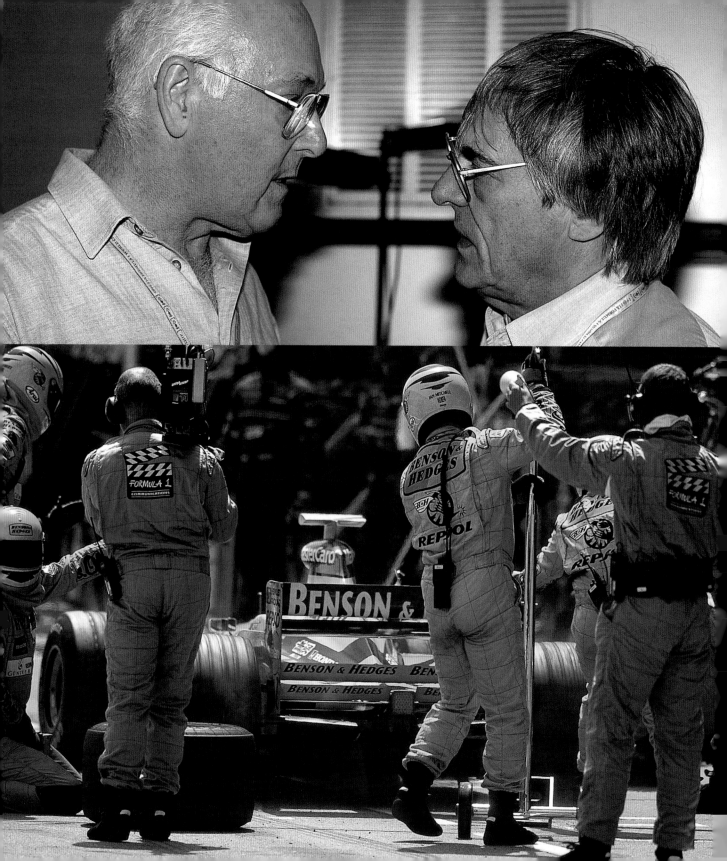

Worldwide TV exposure grows year on year and Bernie Ecclestone has already set in motion the digital revolution.

Many of Ecclestone's hopes for the future expansion of F1's popularity are based on the possibilities offered by pay-to-view digital channels, which will offer much enhanced picture quality and variety to the viewer. With this in mind he has already invested £40 million in a remarkable air-conditioned mobile digital television production studio which has been shipped from race to race across the world since the start of the 1997 season.

However, it remains to be seen whether digital coverage takes off in the way Ecclestone anticipates. There are sceptics who believe that most viewers want their TV coverage packaged and delivered to their screens as a rounded, cohesive product rather than having to dart around with a hand control, making decisions about whether to have a cockpit view from Jean Alesi's car, for example, or watch the refuelling process. The jury is still out on this matter, but its successful resolution is absolutely crucial to the way in which F1's television finances develop over the next few years.

It may also be crucial in guaranteeing the future income of Grand Prix racing's top drivers. Michael Schumacher's current status as the best driver in the F1 business, allied to the global television coverage his Marlboro- and Dekra-bedecked image offers to those two key sponsors, gives him an income of £16 million from his racing activities. Add to that another £10 million from

Under scrutiny; regular media conferences are compulsory in today's publicity-driven F1 environment.

merchandising and the German ace, not yet thirty, could be earning a million pounds for every year of his life during the 1999 F1 season.

By contrast, another former World Champion, Damon Hill, earned around £4 million from the Jordan team in 1998 with perhaps another £500,000 from personal sponsorship and merchandising income of around £2 million. The disparity seems huge but is a fact of life. Further back down the grid, bright-eyed newcomers such as Benetton's Alexander Wurz will earn around £750,000. But their time will undoubtedly come.

It is, however, worth mentioning that television viewers can be very fickle when it comes to Formula 1 racing. In 1997 the BBC lost its coverage of the World Championship when rivals ITV bid £68 million for the series rights over five years. It was a success, but not without its pitfalls, as ITV network director Marcus Plantin explained midway through that first season.

'We bought F1 specifically to attract more men to ITV, and the sport has delivered them in spades,' he said. 'Unlike the BBC, ITV is a commercial channel relying on advertising for its revenue – and F1 has been a huge commercial success for us.

'The number of ABC1 men and 16–34 men – the two demographic groups which are notoriously difficult to get to watch television – had increased by nearly 450 per cent year-on-year on Sunday afternoon.'

Opposite: Damon Hill and wife Georgie enjoy the Grand Prix good life at Jordan, while over at Sauber *(above)* Jean Alesi and wife Kumiko enjoy a rare moment of calm.

Nevertheless, what is popularly known as the 'Damon Hill factor' played a part in a steady drop-off in viewers during the European season. The 1997 San Marino GP saw only 4.2 million viewers switch on to watch Heinz-Harald Frentzen's narrow victory over Michael Schumacher, 800,000 fewer than the number who tuned in to watch Hill's victory in the same race 12 months earlier.

The figures were 1.5 million viewers down for the '97 Monaco GP, 1.6 million down for the Spanish GP, 1.8 million down for Magny-Cours, only 0.6 million down for Silverstone and then 1.8 million down at Hockenheim. Interestingly, the Brazilian and Canadian races – whose live UK screening took place early on a Sunday evening rather than during the afternoon – both registered substantial increases in viewers, while figures for the Argentine GP were unchanged.

'It is very difficult to reach accurate conclusions on these matters,' said Andrew Chown, the man who negotiated ITV's deal with Bernie Ecclestone.

'It is taken for granted that any sports broadcasting will benefit when a British competitor is in contention. But you must remember that we do not compare our own viewing figures with what the BBC did last year – we compare them with what we did with those corresponding slots last year when we were screening a mixture of films, local programmes and acquired series.

'In that respect F1 has been hugely successful, with viewing figures more than four times greater than what we had before. It is always nice to get big ratings – that is the name of the game – but we would have been unwise to rely on the efforts of one man, Damon, when we entered into a five-year agreement. British success represents a bonus for us.'

It will be interesting to see where the 'David Coulthard factor' leaves UK viewership figures at the end of 1998.

David Coulthard leads the field at the start of the 1998 Canadian GP. With the formidable new McLaren-Mercedes at his disposal, the Scot has taken over from Damon Hill as the centre of attention for ITV's armchair viewers.

Overleaf: Right route; Mika Häkkinen's McLaren-Mercedes takes the chequered flag to win the 1998 Spanish Grand Prix.